MW01595946

COPYRIGHT

FOR GOD AND COUNTRY
By Nick Mariano

PROLOGUE

   I should start out by saying that I have been retired more than 20 years after having worked for the United States Government for close to 30 years. As you read some of my accounts and stories you may think to yourself, "This guy is nuts, Special Agents don't do this kind of shit." They'd be disciplined or fired on the spot. Today that would be more than true as we have seen with recent incidents involving government agents being involved in sexual scandals, lack of discipline or not carrying out their duties and having people injured or killed. The stories I'm telling you about happened over 25-30 years ago when the government was a different animal and people did shit that never got reported or we didn't get disciplined for what we did. Those were different times. Terrorism wasn't what it is today. We had demonstrations against embassies overseas, deranged person attacking protected persons and isolated incidents but there was no Taliban or Al Qaeda planning attacks against us. Yes, some of the things we did were stupid when I look back but nonetheless we did them and later laughed about it. I should also say, that despite my stories, the Bureau of Diplomatic Security of the United States Department of State, is now one of the most, if not the most professional, well trained and multi-trained law enforcement organization in the United States Government or in the world.

The Diplomatic Security Service's web site defines our organization as follows:
The Bureau of Diplomatic Security (DS) is the security and law enforcement arm of the U.S. Department of State. DS is a world leader in international investigations, threat analysis, cyber security, counterterrorism, security technology, and protection of people, property, and information. The Bureau is responsible for providing a safe and secure environment for the conduct of U.S. foreign policy. Every diplomatic mission in the world operates under a security program designed and maintained by Diplomatic Security. In the United States, Diplomatic Security personnel protect the Secretary of State and high ranking foreign dignitaries and officials visiting the United States, investigate passport and visa

fraud, and conduct personnel security investigations. Operating from a global platform in 31 U.S. cities and more than 160 foreign countries, DS ensures that America can conduct diplomacy safely and securely. DS plays a vital role in protecting 275 U.S. diplomatic missions and their personnel overseas, securing critical information systems, investigating passport and visa fraud, and fighting the war on terror.

DEDICATION

I dedicate this book to all the Special Agents I have had the honor of working with, many of who have since passed. I also dedicate this book to the new breed of Special Agents now working for the Diplomatic Security Service (DSS) and for the job they are doing in keeping fellow diplomats safe overseas despite the terrorist threat that currently exists and for the work they also do here in the United States, which many times goes completely unnoticed by the average citizen. I think I can be safe in saying that the average citizen doesn't even know our organization exists or have any idea what we do. Many of my friends still think I worked for and continue to work for the CIA despite my telling them that I work for DSS.

THE EARLY YEARS

So how did I get into DS? To answer that I have to go back to 1968. I had just finished college, the Viet Nam War was in full swing and I was eligible for the draft. My friend Frank and I decided it might be wise for enlist in the military since we were probably going to get drafted and we had heard that some of the draftees were going into the Army and some were being put in the Marines. We thought, holy shit, love the Marine Corps as an organization, but we had heard about their boot camp and we wanted no part of that insanity. So Army it was. We took all the different tests the Army gives you and both of us scored very high, at least for folks coming out of Hazleton, Pennsylvania. So we enlisted into the Army with an MOS (specialty) of Army Intelligence. Two weeks later we were off to boot camp at Fort Dix, New Jersey, for our basic training. While I don't want to get into our 9 weeks of training there in full detail, I do have some humorous stories to tell about boot camp.

Most of the guys in my company were college graduates and after a week or two of boot camp we came to view our training as a sort of advanced Boy Scout training. Yes, it was hard and we learned a lot but we also fucked around a lot too. We were up daily at 0500 hrs to the sounds of Mad Dog, one of our drill instructors (DIs) yelling and beating on the garbage can and telling us to get our asses in gear or else. We did the Army stuff during the day but when we got back to the barracks we acted like we were back in college again. We tied people into their bunks. Short sheeted them. Basically fixing their bed by folding the sheets in half so when they climbed into the sack they couldn't get all the way into their sheets. At night we'd designate one unfortunate recruit to take all our money and sneak outside when the pizza wagon came around and buy us pizzas. This was a no-no for recruits and it wasn't like we were starving as the Army did feed us well. That poor sole usually made it outside and back without the DI catching him but occasionally he got caught and faced the wrath of the DI and got down and gave him 100 push-ups. Sometimes we got the same too. If he didn't get caught however, it was always kind of funny when the DI came in the next morning and found a trashcan of empty pizza boxes. Boxes, what boxes?

Our Company Commander was nicknamed Fat Cap by the troops because he was a little on the hefty side but I must say he was a fair and good CO. Many a day we marched to the gun ranges and got caught in a rainy down pour. He could have hopped on the next passing truck and rode back to the barracks but he marched along side his men in the rain and made sure we got something hot to drink when we got back to the barracks. He was also fair in giving us post privileges as we progressed through our basic training. This meant that we could roam the base for a few hours and even get a beer instead of staying in our barracks doing chores. One time I remember though we were expecting a pass to leave the base as basic training was ending and as we stood in formation dreaming of going home or someplace he announced that he was giving us post privileges. That didn't go over very well with the guys and I could hear several guys whisper," Fuck You! Stick those post privileges up your ass, We want a Pass!" Fortunately, neither the CO nor the DIs heard any of that or our asses would have been grass.

Basic training finally ended and Frank and I headed to Fort Holabird, Maryland, the home of the U.S. Army Intelligence Command School. Going from basic training to intelligence school was like going from Boy Scout camp to being back in college and living at a frat house. The first day we arrived there were all sorts of guys in civilian clothes and with Long Hair!

Again almost all the guys in my class were college grads except for our squad leader who was career Army. More about him later. The base was left over from WW II and run down and we were next door to the Colgate Palmolive Plant and a yeast company. Great smells depending on which direction the wind was blowing. Classes were great and we learned a lot although we put in major hours studying but it was like being back in college. The real Army was basically over for us. We were students again and when we were finished we would be spies. Ya, spies. That's the ticket. We did fuck around while at school though. Most of the time the brunt of our pranks was our Career Army Squad Leader. A good guy, but hey, he didn't go to college. So let's fuck with him.

Pranks were funny but not what I consider nasty. We lived in a common area and had bunks just like in boot camp. He however, had his own private 6'X6' private room complete with a window and a door he could close, just in case he wanted to things in private. Anyway, our favorite prank was to tie his door to the door across the hall so that in the morning he couldn't get out of his room unless he crawled out the window. Who tied the door? Beats me. Second best prank, Friday night was head to town and knock back a few beers. Most of us got back way before he did, so we'd put our footlockers (those wooden boxes where we put our personal stuff in and locked everything up with a pad lock) every 3 feet or so across the aisle of the barracks. We knew our fearless squad leader would have to transverse this walkway when he hit the head (bathroom) before he hits the sack. We would lay in compete silence or perhaps fake a snore waiting for him to return home and make his journey to the head. Here he is! He's home! He's in his room for a moment. He's headed to the head. Any minute now. BOOM! Down he goes as he trips over the first of several footlockers that we laid as a trap for him. He's up, he's down. Finally after about the third time that he goes down, he freaks out, yelling, screaming, cursing and yes, flinging the footlockers across the barracks. A few muffled laughs from the guys but nothing loud enough to give away who planted the traps.

Another favorite prank among the guys. Ya, the old tie the guy in his bunk when he's sleeping or better yet, drunk, from a night in old Baltimore. He'd wake up and lo and behold, he couldn't move. Funny. Well, you had to be there. How drunk did we get on weekends? Drunk enough that we could turn a guy's wall locker around so that the back was facing the front and the door was against the wall. Next step. Get a magic marker and draw a door on the backside and then watch some drunk, soon to be Special Agent in Military Intelligence, try to unsuccessfully try to open his locker for half an hour. Again, maybe you had to be there to fully appreciate it. Then there was the time that someone took the cannon from the parade field, rolled it about half a mile down the road and up onto the porch of the Commanding Officer of the entire school so that when he walked outside the next day he was face to face with an old Civil War cannon. Funny, again you had to be there. Is this the Army Intelligence Command or Tapa-A-Keg-A-Day fraternity?

One last event at Ft Holabird that was pretty funny. Actually one funny and one not so funny, depending on how you looked at it. One of our main classes was surveillance. How to detect being followed and how to lose someone if you are. Image this. The class was broken into about 6 groups, each of whom had to follow an instructor without being detected. So off we go to downtown Baltimore, first Fulton's Fish Market and then the infamous Block, home of Blaze Star and other famous strip bars. The instructors had a good sense of humor as they always made sure that all six groups first ended up at the fish market, coming in from all different directions but all ending up at the same spot, where upon all the workers there started to laugh when they realized that it was another practical exercise from the intelligence school. Upon leaving the fish market, all the groups went different ways, each following their designated spy and ending up at a strip club where the instructor advised us that the exercise was over and since we're here, let's have a beer and check out the talent.

The other incident I still remember from the BIRD was our few days at the Viet Cong make believe village where we learned about Viet Nam, since we thought most of us were probably headed there after our training. It was just like the real thing. We did searches and grabbed suspects that could be Viet Cong and then learned how to interrogate these bad guys and get good intelligence. One day we were simulating being in a helicopter with two suspected Viet Cong and learning how to go about interrogating these guys. So the lesson went something like this. The instructor says, "so we have to get intelligence from these guys. How do we get it? First we ask prisoner #1, what do you know about Viet Cong operations? No response. Well, then we grab the guy and throw him out of the helicopter and down to the ground. Next, we say to guy #2, what do you know?" Oh ya, this guy is ready to talk forever. I can't say for certain that our instructor was serious but this was the Viet Nam War!

Before graduation all the MI classes were given money by the Army to have a party to celebrate finishing school. A friend of mine lived in Baltimore and was friends with someone at the Playboy Club He arranged to get us the club for the night of our party. When I went to the Commanding Officer to get the money for the party and told him where it was going to be, he could not believe it. Nor could he believe that neither he nor the First Sergeant was invited to it. He did made it clear to me that I better have the receipt for the party and get it back to him the next morning, first thing or instead of being a Special Agent in MI, I would be a Special Agent washing dishes for the rest of my career in the Army.

Henny Youngman was the comedian at the Club that night and when he found out that we were all new MI Agents he proceeded to bust our ass about how intelligence and the Army didn't go together. A great time was had by all. Free booze, food, Playboy Bunnies and not having to spend a penny. What could be better than that?

So, we finally finished Intelligence School and were now full-fledged Special Agents. So what do we do now? Well, I ended up in Erie, Pennsylvania and a number of my classmates got state side assignments, some got language school like my buddy Frank and a few went overseas but fortunately not to Viet Nam. Our whole class dodged the bullet as far as Nam was concerned since we were certain all of us were destined to go to the war there. I ended up fighting the war in Erie along with another agent who shared the office with me. These were the good old days of Army folks spying on folks in the U.S.A., especially those communist student protestors who were everywhere and at all the colleges.

We went to peace rallies and sang peace songs along with the college students in Erie and although most of the students knew my room mate and I, since we went to all the parties at their houses all the time and dated local girls, we still did our thing.

The funny part about going to the peace demonstrations was that my room mate and I had very long hair, wore blue jeans and T-shirts to the rallies and afterwards wrote whatever reports we were required to.

The other intelligence folks in town also went to the same rallies as us but we always had to laugh when we see them there. Our two friends from Air Force Intelligence, OSI, came to the rallies wearing blue jeans and T-shirts but had crew cut haircuts. Who in the late 60's had crew cut haircuts? Certainly not the students. Then there was the FBI who did the same stuff that we did and they came to rallies too but tended to wear suits, white shirts and ties and sometimes hats. We were able to quickly ID all the Feds since who else wore suits to peace rallies and hung around taking notes and eye balling the crowd.

Then there were the minorities, you know who I mean, who we kept an eye on them and reported on their activities. You know, the good old Black Panthers but I'm not really sure Erie had any of them but we still reported on anyone we considered suspect. This went on for about 2 years and then all of a sudden we, the US Army, was out of the spy business as far as U.S. citizens were concerned. Sixty Minutes did a series of TV shows on Army Intelligence and reported about all the bad stuff we were doing in the U.S. of A against our citizens. One day we got a call from Headquarters Commander and he told us that we weren't going to do that shit any more. No more spying on folks in town. He told me to empty our safes of all the reports we had on the good folks of Erie and take them home and burn everything. That afternoon I packed the government car with everything we were told to get rid of, drove to my house in the countryside, since I lived way outside town by the farms, got out the old trusty burner (you probably don't know what I mean, but back then we have wire type container baskets and we burned trash and newspaper, etc. at home) and commenced to spend the next several hours burning all our office files. After that, we went to work in suits and had regular haircuts and just knocked on doors and did background investigations on potential Army folks who needed a security clearance.

I almost forgot to mention that we got many, what I'll call nut jobs, who came to our office to report everything from UFOs to one guy who found the cure for cancer. I should add that he did so while being on board the Starship Enterprise and working on their propulsion systems. Then we had the guys who thought the government was beaming rays at them and that their minds were being altered and controlled by the government. In these cases we just recommended that the person wrap aluminum foil around his head and told him that he would be safe from all the beams and radiation. Even though this was fairly funny to us, there were still a few scary moments when some 6' plus guy would walk into the office to tell us sometime and we had to control our smiles and laughter for fear of getting the shit kicked out of us. Most times we couldn't resolve the person's problem to his satisfaction and in these cases we recommended that he go up to the next floor in the Federal Bldg. and talk with the guys at the FBI since they always were able to help these people out. I'm sure that when the Bureau found out we were doing these referrals they came to dislike us even more than they did anyway. I'm sure they thought the armed forces of America couldn't do the job as well as they could.

So finally my discharge came through and after several successful applications to the U.S. Government, I decided to go to work for IRS Intelligence.

Yes, that organization that strikes fear into your average citizen. I had been offered jobs with the Pennsylvania Crime Commission, the U.S. Postal Inspectors, the Inspector General of the U.S. Department of Agriculture, the Treasury Department and even sent an application to the U.S. Department of State, which I didn't even know if or what they did but my wife suggested it, so I did it. It turns out they were going through a hiring freeze at the time but they told me they would keep me in mind when the hiring got rolling again.

So off I went to the U.S. Treasury Law Enforcement School in Washington, DC. for about a year of training to be a G-man. Training was great and we learned a lot about the Treasury Department and later what IRS was all about. I don't plan to write a whole lot about the IRS since the job was really an accountant with a gun. Furthermore, I don't want anyone there to get pissed at me and start an audit of my finances.

After school ended I was assigned to the Baltimore Field Office and my boss disliked me from Day One because I still had my long hair from my Army days and I usually didn't wear a white shirt with my suit and tie. This may sound stupid, but let me tell a short story about a friend of mine at IRS, who later left and joined the FBI. He was in class one day and J. Edgar himself came into the class room, looked around and saw two agent candidates with colored shirts on with their suits and tie, and stated and I quote: " I see we have two farmers in the class." Well, next day those fellows weren't in class anymore or still employed by the FBI. Enough said. Getting back to my boss at the IRS, he continually told me to get a haircut and I continually told him I would do so when the bankers and attorneys I worked with did the same. At the time, early 70's, IRS Intelligence Agents didn't carry guns unless the chief had something special for them to do like protecting a presidential candidate during the elections or arresting someone really bad. One day he told my buddy and I to go and serve some Grand Jury subpoenas on some mob guys. We asked him for our guns and he couldn't understand why we would need them. We told him we didn't want to end up in the river with concrete shoes, so he finally gave in and turned over our six shooters. Ya, we carried snub nose 38's, which I wouldn't want to rely on if the shit hit the fan.

Not many exciting stories about this job phase of mine but it was always a hoot when my wife and I went to neighborhood parties and someone asked me where I worked. "Well, I work for the IRS." "Oh, nice to meet you," while they slowly moved away from us least I decide to audit or investigate them for whatever. That was the one cool part of the job. When we were bored at the office, we'd grab the G-ride and drive through low-income neighborhoods looking for those brand new Cadillacs with those big ass chrome front grills on them. When we saw one, we'd write down the license number and saw most times that the guy driving this very expensive car was only making about $1,000 a year according to his tax returns. Time to call him in for a little interview. Want to see someone squirm and start sweating, just call him into the local IRS office to discuss his taxes, but first give him his rights just in case. Heart attack time. Don't get me wrong. We weren't pricks. We did the same thing at boat marinas where we'd find someone who owned a $50,000 boat and was only making

$5,000 a year according to his tax return. Most of the guys we brought in were bad guys, pimps, drug dealers or mob guys. We weren't doing this to Joe-
Q-Citizen.

Other folks we liked to investigate were VIPs. Our office arrested and convicted the Governor of Maryland and later the Vice-President of the United States, Spiro Agnew. Want to get the average citizen's attention, arrest a politician or movie star.

The only other funny thing that happened when I was at the IRS in Baltimore happened one afternoon in late summer. I came into the office and everyone there was standing at the windows facing the street and the Morris Mechanics Theater that was in front of the Federal Bldg. When I finally managed to get a front row seat and see what was happening, I learned that a guy was boning his girlfriend on the upper patio of the theater and having a great old time. The front of the Federal Bldg. was all reflective glass and he didn't realize that about 100 or so federal employees were having a great lunchtime porn show right from their offices.

THE OFFICE OF SECURITY

Well, finally one day I received a call from the U.S. Department of State, telling me that the hiring freeze was over and I had a job with the Office of Security (SY), later to become the Diplomatic Security Service. I quickly resigned from my job at Treasury and reported for duty with the State Department November 1972. When I came aboard with SY there were only about 300 Special Agents and Security Officers worldwide in the organization and most of us came from military backgrounds; Army Military Intelligence, Naval Intelligence or Air Force OSI. During my initial interview with SY the Agent interviewing me asked me if I wanted to come and work for them. I replied, "Yes," and he replied, "OK you've got the job provided you pass the background investigation and medical clearances." That was it! Not much of a screening process but SY was virtually unknown to most people back in the 70's. When people see agents protecting foreign dignitaries they immediately think Secret Service, even though State Department protects a big majority of world leaders. So I came on board in November 1972 and was all set for some great training like the year of schooling I received with the Treasury Department. Wrong! We had a weeklong seminar given by all the Division and Section heads, who told us what SY did and not much about how they did it. When that was done everyone in my class went off to a Field Office; in my case the Washington Field Office, WFO, to start working. Back then the main duties Agents had was doing background investigations and an occasional assignment protecting some foreign dignitary. I should mention that DS is not the same animal now. Agent positions are advertised on our web site on the Internet and during one week we get over 3,000 people applying for the job. These folks are screened and re-screened and the lucky few then get tested throughout the US. The persons that manage to pass the testing are put on an eligibility list, and in a very good year of hiring maybe 20-30 new agents come on board. Currently DS has somewhere near 2,000 Special Agents and Security Officers, a far cry from the 300 we had when I came on. New Agents are then assigned to a Basic Agent's Class and go through at least one year of very diversified training before being assigned somewhere in the USA. Agents going overseas to high threat posts may get an additional six months of training before they deploy. Now don't get me wrong. I did get a lot of training while I worked for DS, but that came later in my career and before many of my overseas assignments.

So I went to the Washington Field Office and was out under the guidance of an experienced Agent for a few weeks before being left on my own to ring door bells and do background investigations throughout the area. Not much fun but that's what we did back then. Nowadays we have contractors doing the bell ringing. Then all of a sudden I was told I was being assigned to the protective detail for the Secretary of State. So I was issued a handgun and a radio, taken out to Vienna, Virginia, and given the opportunity to shoot my new gun in a dirt lot behind some houses and Presto, I was on the Secretary's Detail. Good thing I had been given adequate protective training while I was with Treasury and had protected some Presidential candidates as I had a general idea about what I was supposed to do. My boss told me I was to be at the Secretary's house the next day to start working the detail. I asked, "What am I supposed to do?" The Response, "Don't worry, someone will fill you in tomorrow." Next day I managed to find the Secretary's house in Bethesda, Maryland, and was ready to roll. Back then we didn't have protective details like today. No 40-50 Agents protecting the big guy. We had a limo with a driver and one Agent in the front seat and one follow car with a Marine Security Guard driving and one Agent riding shotgun. My briefing consisted of being told to keep an eye on things and make sure the follow car doesn't lose the limo. Then off we went with me riding in the follow car. Did this for a while and then got promoted to the limo. Again asked, "what do I do?" The response: "Just sit there and DON'T talk to the Secretary unless he asks you something. When we get where we're going, jump out, check things out and get the door open for the Secretary and stick with him. Someone will meet you when you arrive." Sounds easy enough. This may sound pretty bad from a training and security point of view when you look at today's security details, but Hey we never lost a

Secretary and we even prevented a few actual attacks on the Secretary. How? I'm not sure but we did. Stateside we had about 5 Agents on the Secretary's Detail and might bump it up a man or two when we went overseas. I remember my first overseas trip with the Secretary. Korea and then Tokyo and return via Hawaii. Got out to Andrews Air Force Base and there's the Secretary's G-ride. A big old 707 jet complete with all sorts of private rooms and electronic stuff on board. Was told during the pre-trip briefing that there was one Very, Very Important thing to remember when we got to Andrews. MAKE SURE THE SECRETARY'S GOLF CLUBS GET ON BOARD!!! Yes, he was an avid golfer and many a meeting with a foreign head of state was done out on some golf course. I should add that he was a very good golfer to boot. Anyway, we're all on board and the Secretary, Press Corps and Staff is at the front of the plane and the 3-4 Agents and a few Marines are in the rear. The plane takes off, coats come off, we wipe out a smoke (as smoking on planes was OK back then) and then order a scotch and water. Great service provided by U.S. Air Force stewards. About 15 minutes later the Secretary shows up in the back of the plane and asks if anyone wanted to play some poker. And yes, we played for money. So there we sit, jackets off, shoulder holsters and loaded guns on, smoking away, having a few scotches and playing poker with the Secretary of State. Yes, he was a good player, and usually kicked our asses and won all the money. And no we didn't just let him win. Play cards and drink for the greater part of the flight and then just before landing the Secretary thanks us for the game and heads back up front. We get our jackets back on and are ready to protect the Big Guy when we hit the ground. The trip goes well and we spend a few afternoons on golf courses with about 100 or so foreign police running all around the course and following our guy. After we get the Secretary back to the hotel and in for the night and we head out with the local police for a night of drinking before doing it again the next day. As I said at the beginning. This would never happen today as the rules about drinking and number of hours it can be done before you start duty are all fixed firmly in the regulations. Back then, it wasn't so and everyone had a few pops before we got back to business. No one ever got shit faced or embarrassed himself, or the Department, and we did our jobs well and in a professional manner. We got back to DC a few days later and continue doing our thing there.

One sort of funny story, depending on how you look at it, occurred at the Secretary's house where we had a small command post in his garage. Back then we still carried the Thompson Submachine Gun and had one in the command post in case the shit hit the fan. There was always a Marine on duty at the house, whether the Secretary was in town or not. It seems that one night, when the Secretary was out of town, the Marine on duty was either cleaning the Thompson or fucking with it, we never did get the whole story. Anyway, he blows the hell out of the desk in the CP and then instead of telling anyone, he merely covers the desk with the Washington Post and waits until he gets relieved at the end of his shift. He then gets his things together and leaves. The next Marine comes in; folds up the newspaper and voila, there are about a dozen 45-caliber bullet holes in the desk. When the prior Marine was asked about the holes, he said he had no idea how they got there. We were all sure who did it but couldn't really prove it. Like they say, "Cheaters Come to Prove." The guy we thought was guilty wrecks the follow car the next week and we were able to kick his ass off the detail for that Then there was the night that a possum or raccoon set off the perimeter alarm at the house and one of our Agents storms the house fully loaded, only to find the Secretary and the Mrs. asleep in bed. Well, better safe than sorry. The Secretary and his wife were great folks and Mrs. would bring us hot chocolate and cookies many a night while we tried to stay awake in the CP. It was also an adventure when I got to protect just the Mrs. Usually I rode shotgun in her car, which was a 1960 something Cadillac convertible. Talk about bad driving. I don't know how many times I thought we had it as she pulled out in front of traffic while several cars blew their horns in anger. She would usually turn to me and say: "Now what could be their problem?" Jesus woman you just drove in front of a car and cut him off. I would just bite my tongue and replied, "I had no idea." Almost without fail we headed to the Congressional Golf Club when I was with her and upon getting there I was given my marching orders by her. She'd say, "I know you're here to protect me, BUT I don't want to see you while I'm golfing." Good thing the course had LOTS of trees so I could slink around in the woods while trying to hid as she, and usually the Japanese Ambassador's wife, golfed.

I still remember one Saturday night the Secretary and his wife decided to go to Georgetown to see a new movie that just opened, "The Day of the Jackal" If this is before your time, it's a movie about a professional assassin, code named the Jackal, who's trying to assassinate a government head of state. We get to the theater and the Secretary and his wife buy their tickets and go in and my partner and I realize we have no money on us. You have to realize this was way before debit cards came out. So being good Special Agents that we were, we flash our badges and tell the girl at the ticket window we are Feds and going into the theater, ticket or no ticket, to protect the Secretary. We sit through the movie right behind the Secretary and his wife, and on the way out of the theater the Secretary turns to us and says, " If you see any guys with crutches coming toward me you better shoot him before he gets me" and then starts to laugh. We also think it's kind of funny for him to be telling us that. For those who haven't seen this movie, the Jackal dresses like an old man with metal crutches, which are in fact a concerned and specially made rifle.

Just before this Secretary left office to go back into the private sector, he decided to have a party at his house, but only for the Special Agents and Marines who worked on his protective detail over the years. No staff, no VIPs. Just us humps. It was a very nice affair, spouses were invited, and plenty of good food and drinks. The one thing I remember most about this party was that Pringles potato chips had just come out on the market and the Secretary walked around the room offering us some of these brand new Pringle chips. "Hey, aren't these something!"

When my assignment on the Secretary's Detail finally ended and I was assigned to the Protective Intelligence Branch or PIB. Four of us sat in an office at State Department and we were supposed to screen folks coming into the US to make sure they weren't terrorists. "Operation Boulder." Where they got that name beats me but everyday we checked names of possible terrorists and everyday we failed to find any bad guys trying to visit our shores. The Office also performed one other important function. We screened all the NUTS who contacted the Department, Secretary or whoever, either in person, by telephone or by mail. All the nut cases came to us. The telephone, where potential crank calls came into, was appropriately named the "NUT Phone." When the phone rang everyone start to sing, I'm a nut, I'm a nut, I'm a nut, nut, nut. Then we would scramble so that we weren't the closest to the phone that meant you had to answer it. Some calls were legitimate but the majority were people with a definite problem. One caller in particular I remember stayed on the line for well over a hour and when we traced the call back he lived on the other side of the US which meant a Big, Big phone bill since that was before cell phones or Skype. We always answered the phone with a fictitious name so people didn't know who we really were. Mr. Anderson was a popular name as was Mr. Smith. We used a variety of names but usually forgot which ones we had used. This generally wasn't a problem unless someone called back and asked for Mr. Anderson or Mr. Smith and then we'd have to figure out who used that name so that we didn't give the caller the wrong person to talk to. We also screened letters, which sometimes were very funny and other times kind of scary. Walk-ins were also common at the State Department and usually the good ones came in during a full moon. People don't believe me when I tell them that many a great nut case has shown up at the posts I've been assigned to during the full moon. Just something about that old full moon that affects people. Most of the time we could talk to the person and assure him that we would fix something but other times we had to resort to the old aluminum hat therapy when he claimed that the government was beaming rays through his head. Think one time we even had to make a hat for the guy before he agreed to leave the building.

During this period of my career President Nixon started to form a relationship with the Chinese and so began the endless barrage of visiting Chinese groups into the United States on cultural exchanges. For the next year to year and a half I was continually on the road with visiting Chinese groups that included the Chinese Hydro-Technical Engineers, the Chinese Acrobats, the Chinese Medical Doctors, the Chinese Martial Arts guys and a few others that I've forgotten. Even though we were technically protecting the Chinese, we were more of facilitators making sure they got through airport screening without any problems and getting them from point A to point B unmolested. We were also there in case someone decided he didn't like the Communist Chinese, which is how many people still looked upon them, especially when they were walking around in their Mao suits. These trips usually lasted several weeks, in the case of the Hydro-Technical Engineers, 26 weeks, and had us visiting every dam and waterway in the United States from Seattle, Washington, down to the Mississippi Delta. We went on dams, over dams, inside dams, to dams still under construction and explored the Snake River and the Mighty Mississippi. Many a funny thing happened to us on these trips and I'll just touch on some of the funnier things that I can remember.

The Chinese caused quite a scene when they came into some towns wearing their Mao suits, especially in the Deep South. This was something brand new to the American people and some thought of it as a novelty and others still looked upon them as the enemy. The Chinese came to love going to McDonalds for breakfast and lunch and there's nothing funnier than a bunch of Chinese trying to eat eggs over easy with chop sticks. Another favorite of theirs was Disneyland since all the Chinese groups went to Disney World to see Mickey Mouse. We had so many Chinese and other foreign dignitaries going to Disneyland every year that DS had to establish a temporary Resident Office in Orlando, Florida, with an Agent whose sole purpose was to set up tours at Disneyland for all the groups coming through the US. The Chinese loved Disneyland and it was not an easy matter to get them all back on the bus at the end of the day because they wanted to keep going. One of the games the SY Agents would play was called "guess who the intelligence agent is in the group." Not always easy but a good way to pass time while we were waiting for them at a visit stop. Traveling with the Chinese was fun even though our days usually ran from sunrise to sun set and beyond. We enjoyed talking with the members of the group who spoke English and hearing about China and what they thought of the United States.

One funny thing took place in Washington, DC, when my wife and our Afghan Hound, Boris, came to visit me at the hotel as I hadn't been home in almost 22 weeks and communications back then was only by long distance telephone. She and Boris came by the hotel and when the Chinese saw the Afghan Hound they fell in love with him, as dogs were still a rarity in China. One Chinese got so excited that he grabbed the dog and started to hug and caress him, where upon Boris, started to growl and bare his teeth. One of the other Agents quickly got Boris from Mr. Lee's grip before he got his nuts bitten off. Funny now but a potential international incident as the newspapers would probably have carried a feature story reporting that a Chinese VIP was mauled by security officer's Afghan Hound.

We got to work with a big variety of local and state police while on these trips and most were a hoot to work with. They would lead our motorcade and bus along the highways and many a time would hit the lights and sirens and speed down the middle of the road causing on coming traffic to swerve off the road to avoid a head on collusion. When we questioned the police about this technique, they usually said that police vehicles had the right of way on highways and said that's how they did things in the old south. The Agents also managed to hit the gin mills in most of the towns we visited and although several cities in the old south were still dry, we managed to find some private clubs that sold booze under some guise. One club I remember distinctly was the "Propeller Club" in some southern town that was a private club but open to hotel guests and had a big sign with a large pig with a propeller sticking out of his ass. Most of the time we came into these clubs there was absolute silence as most of the folks there knew we were Feds and with the Chinese. Not sure what they thought we were going to do to them but they gave us wide space whenever we showed up.

Many of them even sent rounds of drinks over to us so that we wouldn't arrest them, I guess?

Another humorous event occurred in California when the delegation, our interrupter and I got on the elevator at a large hotel and standing by himself in the rear of the elevator was Colonel Sanders, complete with his snow white suit and string tie. When the Chinese gave him a quick eye, our interrupter said in Chinese to them "The man in the back of the elevator is a very famous person. He sells chickens." Whereupon all the Chinese turned completely around and gave a nervous Colonel Sanders a good looking over.

On my trip with the Chinese Medical Doctors we visited just about every major hospital and health facility in the United States and saw live demonstrations of various procedures and operations that only a doctor can appreciate. During one stop we attended a lecture that started out by the doctor unwrapping a human head before he began his lecture about whatever he was discussing. After the lecture one of the Agents asked one of the Chinese what she thought of the lecture and she responded, "The lecture was very good and the head was very Fresh!" OK. At another hospital stop we decided to wait outside while the Chinese did their thing and got talking with one of the local cops who told us that the doctor they were visiting with was experimenting with head transplants. We said he was full of shit but he insisted that was what this doctor was doing. OK to that too.

During one of the performances of the Chinese Acrobats, someone set off a smoke grenade in the auditorium and so we got the Chinese off the stage while some exited under the front of the stage. One panicked patron tried to exit under the stage too, whereupon my fellow Agent attempted to keep him from following the Chinese into the safe area. This resulted in the patron trying to choke my floor agent, which resulted in him finally getting out his black jack (you know those lead filled leather things that you use to bonk someone with on the head and which most of us still carried in our back pockets at the time) and he gave the guy a good one on the head which quickly brought him back to his senses.

We also ate at several Chinese restaurants while our delegations toured the US, as the Chinese do like Chinese food, even if it's the American version of it. We always had the 12 course affair whenever we went to these as the Chinese are used to ordering an entree a piece and sharing it.

During one of our flights on a very small plane, there were three of us with the Chinese, Don, the Agent in Charge, John and I. John was not a big fan of flying in air planes. The flight took off from Denver or somewhere out west and the pilot puts up the wheels which were right next to our window as the plane had an overhead wing with wheels that hung down by the window. After about 10 minutes the pilot lowers the wheels and the flight still had over an hour to go. This immediately got John's attention and he nervously asked Don why the pilot would be lowering the wheels so soon after take off. Don, who had a very good sense of humor, replied "Oh, that's so when we get to the mountains, the plane can just roll over the tops of the peaks without crashing." This caused John to immediately turn pale while Don and I laughed our asses off.

All trips, regardless of who we were protecting from China, ended in New York City since the Chinese had their official Mission there. New York didn't rank high among the Agents as most New Yorkers could give a rat's ass who you were protecting or what law enforcement organization you worked for. This was New York and it was theirs and people did things the way New Yorkers do things. Case in point. We were trying to park a large tour bus in front of one of the large hotels around Lexington Avenue and my buddy goes over to ask a cabbie to pull up his cab. The cabbie says he is in a hack stand and so he is not going to move. This causes my partner to take out his badge and credentials and reply to the cabbie "Federal Agent, move your cab up a bit" The cabbie's response. "I don't care if you're a fuckin Democrat, I'm not moving my cab." Whereupon one of our NYC Police Officers comes up to the cab and says," New York Police, move your cab up." The cabbie's response, "Fuck you, I'm in a Hack Stand and I ain't moving." This final exchange initiated a physical response by our NYC Police Officer, who was a 6', 200 lbs. person of color. He opened the taxi's door and begin to physically yank the cabbie from the cab while saying" If you won't move the cab, I'll move it." The cab finally gave in, started the engine and began to move up just a bit, when the police officer politely informs him that he better take it around the block.

Another time at the same hotel, my partner goes out on the street to stop traffic so the bus can get out and is almost run over. The guy steps on the gas and my partner gets the old back jack, the same one from the acrobat incident and proceeds to smash the shit out of the guy's windshield, thereby causing the guy to finally take his foot off the gas. In between all these episodes in NYC, the local cops and us usually spent our off time in large hotel rooms, eating, drinking, smoking and playing poker. Not sure what the hotel staff thought when they came into the room and there was a dozen or so guys wearing shoulder holsters and boozing it up while playing cards with a stack of dollars on the table. If you think some of the State Agents were nuts, you haven't worked with New York's BOSI cops, Bureau of Special Investigations. These guys were something else but great to work with. Not sure that organization even exists today.

Then there was the time we were in Boston and decided to have a really nice dinner one evening, complete with some wine. The wine steward, complete with a little silver cup around his neck on a chain, came over to our table and told us about their wines and took our order. A little later one of the junior Agents arrived and sat down. The steward came over again and asked him if he'd like a glass of wine. He replies, " I'll take a glass of Ripple." At this point most of us break up laughing but the wine steward keeps his cool and merely replies, "Might I suggest Monday's vintage, that was a particularly good day."

All Chinese details ended with a large Chinese dinner for everyone, including the Agents, at the Chinese Mission in NYC. This was a multi-course meal that lasted forever and had a fair share of good French wine, Chinese Beer and Chinese liquor called Maotai. The dictionary defines Maotai as follows: Moutai or Maotai is a Chinese liquor, a sauce-scented brand of baijiu. Maotai is distilled from fermented sorghum and now comes in different versions ranging in alcohol content from the standard 53% by volume down to 35%. Yes, you are reading this correctly. 35% to 53% alcohol. Isn't that really kerosene or gas we're talking about? So the dinner typically started out with the Chinese serving the Agents various dishes to include stuff you would get at your average Chinese restaurant plus shredded jellyfish, sea anemone, sea slugs, pickled octopus, plus a few other dishes that we had no idea what they were. So we start to eat and then the Chinese insist that we try the sea slugs, shredded jellyfish, 100-year-old eggs since they are real delicacies and even the Chinese delegation members don't get these foods back in China. So, not to be rude, we eat a few of the delicacies and they ask us how they are and of chose we have to answer "Very Good." Whereupon they continue to fill our plates with more of these goodies over our protests. In between, the Chinese love to do toasts and so during an average meal there were 10-20 toasts, mainly because I think they wanted to get all the Agents drunk and shit faced. During the toast everyone had to yell gānbēi and then down the drink. Every time there a toast, the Agents would reach for the good French wine or Chinese beer but the Chinese insisted that we had to use the Maotai for the toast. They weren't drinking it but we had to. Let me tell you. This shit is evil. It smells like hell as you bring it up to drink and once you get it past your nose and drink it; it is what the American Indians probably called "Fire Water." The stuff burned all the way to the stomach and after a few shots you were well on your way to a bad drunk. By the conclusion of the dinner we were stuffed and pretty much three sheets to the wind (Drunk). Then to top things off, we usually weren't done with our shift and so upon leaving the dinner we got back in our G-ride and sat there until our relieve arrived at midnight. These were not good times as we were hung over and felt like we either had to shit or barf or both and were stuck in the car for another 3-4 hours.

We also went into the Chinese Mission during our stays in NYC as the Chinese were always having meetings there. The Agents sat in a little anti-room off the lobby and we usually got served coffee or tea. We'd sit around and joke and sometimes laugh about the Chinese until an incident happened one day. We were sitting around, smokin and jokin and one of our guys says, " Boy, I wish I had some milk and cookies." Well, about two minutes later one of the service staff at the Mission comes into the room with a tray of milk and cookies. We all looked at each other and then the tray of cookies and silently think to ourselves, "The Chinese wouldn't bug this room so they could hear what we were saying, would they?" So after that day and on future trips to the Mission, there was no more smokin and jokin, at least about the Chinese anyway.

Then there was the Special Agent in Charge (SAIC) of the New York Field Office who wanted to be involved in all these protective details but didn't know shit about how they worked. He was so bad that the folks at JFK Airport had banned him from coming there if there was a VIP arrival. Came across some photos from the Chinese details that reminded of another funny story. I almost forgot to tell you the famous or infamous red bellbottom pants story. Back then we were still wearing bellbottom pants and I had two pair that I loved to wear. A subdued pair of blue check bellbottoms and a pair of bright red bellbottoms with yellow and black checks. I wore the red ones the first time I met my wife's parents before we got married and I thought my future mother-in-law's eyes would pop out when she saw them. The first thing out of her mouth was "Nice Pants." Anyway, I loved these pants for some reason and despite snide remarks from people I kept them and continued to wear them. In fact I even took them with me on my first Chinese Protective Detail. I come out of the hotel one morning and Don, our SAIC, looks at them and me and says "Nice pants, BUT don't wear them on duty anymore." We then both break out laughing. About 3-4 days later I decide it's red pants day again and wear them to work. When I get outside Don sees me and says, "I thought I told you not to wear those pants again to work." I respond, "I thought you were just joking." Don responds, "I wasn't joking! DON'T wear those fuckin pants again. I don't want to see those fuckers again on this trip or else." So the red bellbottoms got banished to my suit case the rest of the trip although I did continue to wear them at home despite my wife's dislike of them also. They have since gone to that big recycle in the sky.

After about 15 months of continual travel I finally got back to Washington, DC, after doing 3 back-to-back Chinese trips all over the United States. This was really something as before these trips about the only states I had ever been to were Pennsylvania, New Jersey, New York, Maryland and Virginia. Thanks to these trips I got to see a lot of the US and got paid while doing it. Back then there was no scheduled overtime or law enforcement pay; it was salary and straight overtime. Between my first two Chinese trips I got over 800 hrs. of paid overtime and that was after we cut out several hundred hours after my boss balled me out for submitting 530 hrs. on my first trip. When you work 7 days a week, sunrise to sunset, for 26 weeks, you tend to get a lot of OT.

Now I'm back in the old Protective Intelligence Branch, doing Operation Boulder and talking with the nuts again on the nut phone. In between all this work the guys in the office decided we needed a distraction so we started to shot rubber bands at each other. To make it even more interesting we called the rubber bands "Murray" and the really big rubber bands a "Big Murray" So we spent hours on end trying to catch each other off guard and then blasting him with a Murray or better yet a Big Murray. Occasionally the boss would catch us and we'd get hell but this game play continued for several months. Might sound dumb but we still had fun when we did it. It must have been the kid in us?

ASSIGNMENT ISTANBUL

So one day my boss walks in and calls me into his office. He says, "How would you like to go to Istanbul on assignment?" Shit, I didn't even know I was eligible for an overseas assignment. So naturally I immediately said, "YES"and he said, "OK you got it." I immediately left his office and ran to the wall map we had hanging in the office and asked my coworker where the hell Istanbul was, as I had absolutely no idea. After a few minutes of searching we finally found Istanbul or Constantinople, as it had been called, and I knew I was headed to Turkey.

We arrived in Istanbul, Turkey, in 1974 and immediately set about trying to find a house to live in. In Turkey houses that are For Rent have large "Kiralık" sign in their windows and so you knew the place was available. The only problem we found was that many of the apartments sat on the sides of hills and were only visible from a great distance or from the lower road. That meant that it often took several hours to figure out where an actual apartment was, as you were driving a few streets away while looking. After some extended searching through the streets of Istanbul we finally gave up on finding a new residence and instead took the departing Administration Officer's house which was located quite a distance from the Consulate General and up towards the Black Sea. It was a single home on a hillside and came complete with goatherds coming through our back yard at different times of the day.

We had been in the house about two days when we were burglarized. It was late at night and Boris, our Afghan Hound, started to bark and bark. We woke up, told him to shut the fuck up and went back to sleep. The next day I got up and went to put on my brand new sneakers and couldn't find them. Went downstairs looking for them and noticed our Sony shortwave radio was also gone. About this time I began to figure that we might have been robbed but after walking through the house once or twice I couldn't see how anyone might have gotten in. All the doors and windows were still locked although we had failed to close and lock the outside metal shutters that covered the doors and windows. Finally I found that someone had cut out one of the window panes, removed it and then took the window with him for fear that he might leave a fingerprint and get arrested. Fortunately we hadn't gotten our household belongings yet so all the burglar got were my new shoes and our radio. From that day forward we faithfully locked all our shutters at night and whenever Boris started to bark we told him to KILL! That caused him to run through the house and if there was a burglar lurking, to scare the shit out of him as Boris was one mean mother if he wanted to be.

Turkey was great. It was a country filled with history, old buildings and the covered bazaar, where we spent endless hours bargaining for carpets, gold and antiques. We got to know all the merchants and became regulars, which meant that they only screwed the tourists and not us. We learned how carpet dealers made carpets look a hundred years old. How jewelers made rubies a brighter red. How the copper merchants took a brand new copper pot and aged it a hundred years so they could sell it as an antique. The covered bazaar became our home away from home. We went there almost every Saturday looking for bargains and drinking tea with the merchants. The merchants got to know us so well that they would even give us carpets to take home and "Live With" before we decided to buy them.

The food and restaurants were also a treat. The great thing with Turkish restaurants was that they would bring the cold and hot appetizers, MEZE, out to your table and you just looked and pointed at whatever you wanted to eat for starters. Next came the main courses, meats or fish, followed by coffee, after dinner drinks and dessert. Your average meal lasted at least 3-4 hours of eating, drinking, smoking and just talking about whatever. If you traveled outside the big cities and couldn't communicate with the restaurant folks, you eventually would be led into the kitchen and they would show you what was cooking in the pots on the stove and you'd just point to what you wanted. The Turks were great people. We learned some basic Turkish but not enough to do much besides eat and get gas. When we attempted to get directions from someone and they saw that we didn't understand them, they'd climb into their car and motion for us to follow them. They'd sometimes drive 5 miles or more just to get us to where we were going. You won't see that happening in the USA very much or ever.

The Consulate General was located downtown on a one-way street and in an old building, which was reportedly the former house of a rich Turkish merchant at some time in the past. Rumor had it that someone had died or been killed in the building and that the place was haunted. I know the Marine Security Guards truly believed this as they said they heard all sorts of strange noises late at night when they were the only ones in the Consulate. I thought this was bullshit until one night when I stood watch for the Marines when we were having their yearly Marine Ball. As I stood at the guard post I heard some weird sounds coming from the upper floors but restrained myself to go upstairs to investigate matters for fear of running into the spirit roaming the building. We also found out later that one of the ceiling paintings in the Consul General's Office had previously been painted over by one of the former Consul Generals when that office was used a bedroom and part of his living quarters. It seems that this Consul Generals spouse got nervous at night looking up at the paintings on the ceiling and seeing all sorts of people looking down at her. Later we learned that several of the doors throughout the building were solid Cherry wood and had also been painted over in white paint.

The Foreign Service back in the 70's was a party animal and it was rare that a weekend went by when we didn't have a party at either the Marine House or someone's home. Work hard and party hard. Many a

Friday the whole consulate would converge on the Marine House for Happy Hour or TGIF and we'd drink, dance, play darts, play pool and party until well into the early morning hours. Usually the Brits and Australians joined us and we usually hit their Consulate's bar whenever something was going on there. Unfortunately the Foreign Service isn't this way now and usually when 5 p.m. comes, people head home and do their own things. Not so back then when I was overseas, as it seemed that everyone worked so they could party.

A few months after we had arrived in Istanbul the Turks invaded Cyprus and everyone in Turkey was convinced that the Greeks would eventually attack Turkey in retaliation. Windows in all business, houses and diplomatic facilities had to be covered at night least the Greeks fly over and find Istanbul and bomb it. Covers were placed on everything. Automobiles had to have blue head light covers and most people were not allowed out on the streets after dark unless they had a special permit. The Turks greatest fear was that the Greeks would bomb the newly completed Bosphorus Bridge, which connected Europe with Asia. To prevent such an attack the Turks positioned a lowly Army private underneath the bridge with a pre-WW II anti-aircraft gun to counter any aerial attack by the Greeks. Everyday as I drove to work I saw this lonely PFC busily cutting down tree branches and placing them strategically around his gun so that if planes flew over and they wouldn't spot him. Unfortunately the gun was so old that by the time he cranked the thing up, Greek jets would have made several passes over the bridge and departed. Luckily the Greeks never attacked and the bridge was safe until the next conflict.

My wife I been told by some Consulate spouses that the first thing one had to do during such a crises was to fill the bath tub with water least the water be shut off at some time. This she did and when I got home she proudly told me what she had done and then took me to the bathroom to show me. The tub was completely empty as all the water had leaked out over the course of a few hours. I did however give her an "A" for trying. She was also told to buy and wear a much gold as you could carry so that if you had to evacuate the country quickly you would have the price of a plane ticket around your neck. This she also did as instructed as evidenced by the gold still in her jewelry box to this day.

At the same time this was going on, a retired Turkish Colonel, who I later became great friends with, was busy forming guerrilla groups among the many villages on the Asian side of the Bosphorus in case the Greeks tried a land assault against Turkey. This never happened but the Colonel became a folk hero as a result and much endeared among the Turkish villagers in the remote parts of Turkey. Several months later, the Chief of Police, who worked on diplomatic matters, invited myself and the Marine NCOIC at the Consulate General to accompany him and the Colonel on a wild boar hunting trip down by Izmir, Turkey. One Friday afternoon off we went to met our friends in my trusty Ford Pinto, which I had brought over from the US. We weren't too sure how to get there and this was before the day of the GPS but we figured it couldn't be that hard as there weren't very many major highways in the country at the time. When we

41

came to the Gallipoli Peninsula and the famous Dardanelles (the spot where the Turks wreaked havoc on the Australians during WW II) we found out that we had to cross the straits on a local boat, which was a hair bigger than my Ford Pinto. I carefully inched the Pinto down two wooden 2X4s and onto the boat and had at least 3-4" to spare on either side. Fortunately the crossing was uneventful and we reached the other shore and managed to move my Pinto off the boat and back onto dry land. A few hours later we were met by the Police Chief and the Colonel, who had gone ahead of us to prepare for the hunt and gather all the village hunters from several villages in the area. In total there were perhaps 50-60 village hunters with their dogs and a wide array of weapons. We spent the night in one of the villages, which just so happened to be having a wedding that night. The villagers decided it would be a great honor to have the foreigners attend their festivities and so we were given the VIP treatment. So we joined the party, ate, drank, danced and at the appropriate times fired our guns into the air in celebration. This was a very Turkish tradition that was carried out throughout Turkey, to include inside the major cities. It wasn't unusual to read in the paper that celebrators at a local hotel had blown the hell out of the ceiling in some ballroom during a wedding party there. We partied well into the night at the wedding and then bright and early the next morning headed out on our boar hunt. Having never hunted boar before, or for that matter even seen a wild boar, I had no idea what they looked like but assumed they were like one of our pigs back home. You also have to realize that this was the first time I or several of my DS friends had ever ventured overseas.

Each of us was assigned a village hunter and several other hunters and their dogs began to drive through the woods to move the boars towards us. You could hear the dogs howl and bark throughout the woods, changing their pitch as they drew closer to the boars. Each time the pitch changed, my local hunter would gesture to me to follow him and we moved to another spot He would then point to a small opening in the woods indicating that is where the boar would be coming through. This went on for quite awhile while the dogs came closer and closer to our hiding spot. I began to wonder how the hell this guy could tell what was happening just by listening to the dogs but low and behold, all of a sudden there was rapid movement ahead of me and I knew the boar was coming. I expected him to come waddling through the opening and stand there so that I could kill him with little or no effort. Instead, this 3' high wild pig came storming through the woods and by the time I get my shotgun up, he is long gone down the path. I should add that boar hunting in Turkey was only permitted with shotguns loaded with 4-buck, no rifle slugs or rifles although I did have my .357 pistol with me. The hunters previously warned us not to get in the path of one of these creatures least he run between our legs and gore the shit out of us. After several hours in the woods we finally managed to bag a few wild boar and were ready to collect them and head back to the village and my car. We just assumed that the Turkish hunters would haul the pigs back for us. We quickly learned that the Turks had no problem hunting wild boar as the boar dug up their crops and were a nuisance in most villages but as most Turks were Muslim they could not touch or eat them. This was grounds for divorce

43

should hunter handle or touch one. So the gunny and I grabbed the nearest pig, which weighed I would guess about 150 lbs. and off we headed back to the village. After about an hour and after being told we have perhaps another hour to go, we tossed this boar on the side when we came across one that weighed only about 100 lbs. After a few hours of trekking through the woods we managed to get our pig back to the village. Our plan was to take him back to Istanbul and have a pig roast the following weekend at my house with all the Marines and security staff. So we're back at the car and realize that since the Turks can't touch the boar they sure as hell they can't gut and clean him for us. I turn to the gunny as I was sure a US Marine could gut a pig and learned that he, like myself, had never hunted anything the large before and so we had to come up with a game plan. I had seen my father clean small animals before and an occasional deer so I decided to take out my knife and give it a try. Got him gutted and then we decided we should skin him while we were at it and so after an hour or so he was ready to be placed on top of the faithful Pinto's luggage rack for his trip back to Istanbul. Again we had to catch the car ferry, I mean that little wooden boat, and carefully drive onto it for our return trip across the Dardanelles, hopefully without driving the Pinto over the boat's edge and into the drink. That done, we finally made it back to Istanbul and got the pig packed into the refrigerator at my house to await roasting the next weekend. The following weekend we roasted that guy and everyone from the office, including our Muslim friends, showed up for beer and wild boar. I got a spit from the Marines and cooked him up and after everyone was done I took the caress back into the kitchen. What happened next was kind of funny. There are endless amounts of cats roaming around Turkey. We had a number of cats that lived in our neighborhood and there were hundreds that roamed the streets of Istanbul. Anyway, after the caress got back to the kitchen and left on the counter top, I decided at one point to grab some more beers and upon entering the kitchen found two cats trying to drag the caress of the boar through a hole they had made in our kitchen screen door. They almost made it as they had the pig three quarters of the way through the screen when I caught them and I managed to reclaim what was left of our meal. Not sure where our dog Boris was during all of this but the cats managed to avoid him somehow.

As I mentioned before, we partied a lot and had all of Turkey to explore which is a beautiful country rich in history and tradition. Most people don't realize just how much history is rooted in Turkey. It's not just the Blue Mosque, Topkapi Palace, the Covered Bazaar or the many forts around the country. Hannibal died and was buried in Turkey, Mount Olympus is in southern Turkey, the House of the Virgin Mary is also in southern Turkey, there is the underground city the Christians lived in at Nevsehir when they were being persecuted by the Turks and the famous ruins of Ephesus are one of the largest ancient ruins in the entire world. There were also those special places that are off the tourist map place where we liked to travel to on summer weekends. Polonezky was a Polish village that has been a part of Turkey for over 170 years. The sultan had given the land to the Poles who were fleeing persecution by the Russians. The village still stands unchanged and Polish is still spoken by its inhabitants. When my mother-in-law, who speaks Polish, went with us to visit the village, she was able to carry on conversations with some of the villagers. What made visiting here a fun thing was that you could drive out to the village, go up to almost any house, find the owner and tell him you'd like to have lunch, whereupon he invited you onto the porch, where you sat while the family prepared your meal. A few minutes after placing your order you usually heard some loud chicken sounds and the sound of an axe taking some chicken's head off. About an hour later a great homemade family style dinner was served to you on the porch. Afterward you strolled through the village and looked at the many old buildings there before heading back to Istanbul.

The Consulate General also had a large motorboat, the Hiawatha which was donated to the Embassy by a former Ambassador. The boat came complete with a captain and two crewmembers and was available to use by Consulate members for a small fee and lunch for the crew. The captain took us to either the Black Sea or the Aegean Sea, where we could swim and picnic on the boat. The boat was firebombed by terrorists a number of years after I left Turkey but I understand that private funds were raised to repair it.

Speaking of terrorists, we had a few incidents at the Consulate however, terrorism was a minor thing overseas in the early 70's. We had a number of demonstrations against the United States or the Turkish Government and occasionally when the crowds got out of hand the police responded with tear gas or rifle fire but nothing major took place during my tour in Istanbul. One night however, someone did throw a small bomb over the wall that landed right next to one of the Consulate drivers as he was getting out of his car. The driver thought someone had thrown garbage over the wall and so he kicked the bag and then turned back to lock his vehicle. A second later there was a small explosion as the detonator, which had been dislodged from the main charge, went off scaring the hell out of the driver but not producing the explosion the guilty party had expected.

Another interesting story occurred when I received a telephone call from the gunny's wife about 2:30 in the morning. She said the gunny was laying on the floor and in extreme pain and didn't know what to do. My wife and I immediately headed up the street to see what was wrong. When we arrived the gunny was rolling around on the floor obviously in agony. Having no idea what was wrong with him, we decided that the gunny and I should head into town in the trusty Pinto to seek medical aid. There was a British Hospital somewhere downtown somewhere although we had only a slight idea about where it was actually located. Again, no GPS or iPhone with Siri, to get you there. So we get down town and I start driving through the maze of streets and see what definitely was a hospital with its Red Cross displayed outside but it didn't look very British. Turns out it was a Turkish hospital and we figured a Turkish hospital was better than no hospital, especially since we didn't know if the gunny was dying or not. So in we go. We meet a nurse and since we didn't speak very much Turkish and she speaks no English, we use gestures to indicate that the gunny had extreme pain in his stomach area. W get into the doctor, who also speaks no English. He looks at the gunny and says" Oh Yoy, Yoy." and leaves. Gunny and I look at each other and wait. A few minutes later the same doctor and the same "Oh Yoy, Yoy." This goes on for about half an hour while the gunny does the funky chicken on the floor or in his bed. Finally we get in touch with more folks from the Consulate who convey the problem and the doctor is done Oh Yo Yo-ing and gives the gunny something for what turned out to be a kidney stone. The gunny finally passed the kidney stone while at the hospital and we were able to finally get him back home.

One of the big news events that took place while I was assigned to Istanbul was the escape of Billy Hayes. For those of you who don't recognize the name, Hayes was arrested at Istanbul Airport in 1970 while trying to smuggle 2 kilos of hashish unto the plane. He was caught when police did a search of him at the airport as the level of terrorism was high at that time. He was sentenced to a very long term in a Turkish prison. These events were later captured in a movie "The Midnight Express." Turkish prisons are something you want to avoid at all costs as they are very different from prisons in the US. The movie depicts the Turkish guards as savage people, which I'm sure some were. What the movie didn't point out was that there were numerous signs posted at Istanbul Airport at the time of Hayes' arrest that advised people that it was ILLEGAL to smuggle or carry drugs on one's person in Turkey and that the consequences were severe. I can't feel sorry for someone who gets arrested after being forewarned about how the Turks felt about drugs. Back to my story. Hayes was visited regularly by Consulate personnel from the time he was arrested and although the US Government did try to get his sentence reduced or help him to back to the United States, the Turks would have nothing to do with that. I still remember to this day going to the weekly Country Team meeting in the Consul General's office sometime in September 1975 and having the CG inform us that Billy had somehow managed to escape and was believed to be headed to Greece. This made sense since I was sure the Greeks would never turn him back over to the Turks, who they disliked at the time. Sure enough, 3 weeks later on October 4, 1975, Billy was reported to have reached Greece and shortly thereafter was on his way back to the US. A number of years later I watched the movie "The Midnight Express" in the US and just shook my head as the whole movie made him out to be a martyr who was being unjustly persecuted by the Turks and portrayed them as monsters who just enjoyed beating the shit out of him. Some of this may have been true but laws are laws and Hayes broke the law in Turkey and should have known that prisons there would be no cakewalk.

Turkey, and Istanbul in particular, is famous for its shopping and my wife and her friend Vernice spend endless hours traversing the country and the cities buying gold jewelry, Turkish carpets, copper and brass, and whatever else struck their fancy. During some shopping trip they were busily bargaining with a merchant, as you never paid what someone asked as the price was in Turkey. This particular merchant didn't appear to speak any English and Vernice spoke very passable Turkish and continued to bargain with the merchant, finally arriving at what my wife thought was a really low price for the item in question. When my wife's asked Vernice how she ever managed to get the item for such a low price, she replied" I leaned forward while I was bargaining with him so he could see my tits." Both she and my wife began to laugh at about the same time the merchant replied something back to Vernice in perfect English. My wife still laughs about this story and the adventures she and her friend had for our two years in Turkey.

As I mentioned, the restaurants in Turkey were fantastic and in the two years we were there we never got sick from eating any food including frequently buying food from street vendors. One restaurant in particular was our favorite and was located a short distance from the Consulate. Rejans Restaurant, located at Olivya Passage in Beyoğlu, was famous for hosting Atatürk's meeting in Istanbul when he ruled the country. In addition, it received distinguished guests from the world of culture and arts such as Agatha Christie, Muhsin Ertuğrul and İbrahim allı. Furthermore, foreign embassy members, Istanbul's rich merchants, wealthy minorities, high-level civil servants, poets, intellectuals, academics and students frequented the restaurant as well. Rejans was founded by two Russian women who reportedly used the building as a brothel in their younger years but later changed it over to a restaurant serving Russian fare when their beauty began to fade. Rejans' specialty was lemon vodka and their famous chicken Kiev ski along with other fantastic Russian dishes. I recently read that Rejans remained opened for over 76 years until it finally closed in 2009, although a move is a foot to reopen it. Another restaurant the diplomatic corps frequented regularly was

Fischers, which I see is still open in Istanbul. Fishers was famous for its schnitzel, which completely filled your plate. This was besides all the other great restaurants in town and those located all along the Bosphorus. Fish restaurants were particularly good as the fish was caught daily, although back in the 60's and 70's the fishermen sometimes got their fish by throwing sticks of dynamite into the water and waiting for the dead fish to surface. An entire swordfish would usually be seen hanging outside the restaurants further out of town and when the fish was ordered by someone, the cook came outside and chopped off a chunk of the fish. As I mentioned, meals were a casual affair. We expected to be in a restaurant for dinner at least 3 hours or longer. Not like today in the U.S. when we're in and out in less than an hour or less. It was a time to smoke, drink, talk and enjoy the various courses of food that Turkish meals consisted of. The appetizers, Meze, were brought out on trays and presented to you so that you could select what you wanted, first cold Meze and then hot Meze. Most of the times you could tell what the food was but other times things you picked turned out not to be what you thought. I remember one time when my wife and I picked out a nice looking deep fried item but weren't sure what it was but it looked fairly appetizing. As we started to eat it, it was like eating deep fried air or maybe water. After some decision and a further analysis we came to the conclusion that it was deep fried brains. At the conclusion of the dinner we finished up with traditional Turkish coffee and one of the many liquors. The Turks produced a wide variety of liquors and soft drinks based on whatever fruits were in season at the time. The same was true of fruit juices that came out as the

51

fruits came into season and were bottled in individual bottles and sold by the case at the local markets.

As I mentioned, there was a wide variety of street vendors who sold kebabs, deep-fried mussels, sweets and other Turkish delights as you roamed through the streets of the city. Also seen around town was the sucu, a waterman, who carried water in a large silver container on his back and poured you a drink of water for a small fee. While we're on the topic of food, we met continuously at each other homes for dinners and parties and besides our own staff we were very close to the Brits and Australians who were real party people. One dinner in particular sticks in my mind at an Aussie's house where he served up some Indian curry. He advised us that he had three levels of the curry: Hot, Medium and Normal. Not being wimps, most people opted for either the Medium or Hot, my wife and I chose the Hot. All I can say is that he wasn't shitting us when he said it was HOT! That curry burned all the way down and each mouthful required about half a bottle of beer to keep from burning up. After the meal was completed, everyone began and continued to blow their noses for several hours. The host Aussie remarked that this was the sign of a truly good curry, when everyone continues to blow their nose long after the meal is done.

Before I leave our assignment in Turkey I have to talk about our Ambassador to Turkey, who was located at our embassy in Ankara, Turkey. The American diplomats had fondly named him "Wild Bill" as he would call you into his office and chew your ass out one moment and the next minute hug you and be your best buddy. He frequently came to Istanbul for meetings and always made a point of going to the weekly Happy Hours at the Marine House. One day I was talking to him in the parking lot of the Consulate and he opened the glove box of his limo to proudly display a .38 caliber Chief's Special that he had. He told me, "See this. Those terrorists aren't going to get me, at least not before I get some of those Fuckers." He was also famous for walking everywhere much to the displeasure of his Turkish bodyguards. Suddenly he would abruptly tell the driver to stop the car, get out of the limo and start walking back to the Consulate, Embassy or his Residence. This drove his Turkish protective detail nuts, as they also had to jump out of their cars to follow him on foot. The Ambassador was famous for being a lover of animals and especially stray dogs. He would think nothing of seeing a stray dog on the streets of Ankara and tell his driver to pull over and fetch the animal. The stray was then taken to the military vet in town and later became a member of his pack of dogs that lived at the Residence. One summer I was assigned to Ankara to fill in for the security officer there and was given the chose of staying in the security officer's house or the Ambassador's Residence, while he was back in the US on consultations. That was a no brainer. Naturally my wife and I chose to stay at the Residence, complete with its service staff and multitude of rooms. We could pick a new room every night to spend the evening. The Ambassador left behind the dog pack and we had our Afghan Hound with us, who romped around with the 20 some dogs who were permanent residents of the Ambassador's House with its sprawling grounds.

The Ambassador's favorite dog however, was a Beagle named Benjamin who went with the

Ambassador almost everywhere. He even could be seen at the Embassy and when it was time for him to head home the Ambassador would dispatch the limo for Benjamin to catch a ride back to the Residence where there was a Marine Security Guard stationed. The Marine would usually get a radio transmission saying the limo was en route, however, no one would advise him that the Ambassador was not in it. The Marine would stand at attention as the limo wheeled into the drive and immediately run to open the car door only to have Benjamin jump out and walk casually into the Residence. Speaking of the Marine Guard at the Residence. The Marine was stationed there 24 x 7 and was responsible for the Ambassador's safety while he was at home. One of Wild Bill's favorite pass times at night was to sneak up on the Marine and try to surprise him or catch him sleeping. This resulted in the Marine getting the shit scared out of him at various times during the night. Fortunately however, the Marine never pulled out his weapon and shot the Ambassador. But back to the Ambassador and Benjamin. As I mentioned, Benjamin was the love of the Ambassador's life, maybe even more beloved than his wife. One time I boarded a plane to make sure the Ambassador was situated OK on board, only to find the Ambassador in his First Class seat with Benjamin sitting right next to him. The Ambassador's spouse was seated one row back.

The Ambassador was a great guy in my eyes and although I only worked with him briefly in Ankara and saw him whenever he came to Istanbul, he tended to remember people. Several years after I left Turkey I received a promotion and Wild Bill shot me a very nice letter congratulating me. I will always remember him for that, as most of my current bosses at the time in DS didn't ever send congrats to me.

One highlight of our tour in Turkey was a visit from my parents. Although my mother probably could have lived without leaving the USA and visiting Turkey, my father was already a world traveler, having served over 18 years in the U.S. Navy and as they said back then, "Join the Navy and see the World", which he did. My father would take our dog Boris for walks almost every day and be gone several hours to the point where we were ready to send out a search party. Usually when he got back he had numerous stories of the places he had gone and the people he had met and talked to. Mean while poor Boris would just lie there panting away and completely exhausted. My father could meet more people during his visits than I ever met while living in a particular country for 2-3 years. While in Istanbul he struck up a friendship with a young prince from Lebanon who was renting a house just down the street for the summer. While the war in Beirut was raging on, several wealthy people from there came to Istanbul to visit and also to drink and live it up at the night clubs before they headed home and to be good Muslims again. My dad visited the prince daily for afternoon tea and at the conclusion of his visit was giving a standing invitation to visit the prince if he ever came to Lebanon.

My father, who was quite the athlete and on the Navy's long distance swimming team and their fleet boxing team, decided that he would join the Marines from the Consulate on their yearly swim across the Bosphorus at one of the narrower stretches. Not only did he complete the swim but he was well ahead of most of the Marine Security Guards. We later found out that he was the oldest person to have ever accomplished this feat. He became an instant hit among the Marines and the local newspaper back home carried the full story of his accomplishment in Turkey. Dad also became a hit at the many parties he attended during his visit. He was usually one of the last people to leave a party and only after I threatened to leave him behind and make him walk home would he agree to leave.

I almost forgot our trip one weekend with some friends to Sofia, Bulgaria, while we were stationed in Turkey. The drive wasn't too bad, only a few hours from Istanbul. We had been told by some friends that if we got stopped by the traffic police in Bulgaria, we should present our American Express card rather than our Diplomatic Passports, as then the police would forget the violation and let us go on our way. We also had to exchange dollars for Bulgarian currency at the border, the Lev and Stotinki, which we thought was very funny for some reason. Upon leaving the country at the end of our weekend we decided we would convert the Stotinki back to Turkish Lira at the border but quickly found out that the Bulgarians didn't want their currency back. They told us that we should change it back on the Turkish side of the border. The Turks, however, said they didn't want the worthless Stotinki either. So there we sat with a pocket full of Bulgarian money that no one, including the Bulgarians, wanted. Just give us your American Express cards!

Downtown Sofia wasn't very big but it was interesting with all the old Communist Party buildings and old Greek Churches. Most of the roads in town had been closed to car traffic so you could walk freely around the streets without worrying about getting run over by some bad Bulgarian driver. Late at night large water trucks came into town and young women in mini-shirts and knee high boots would hose down the streets. The first time I saw this at night I just about broke up especially since mini-skirts were no longer in fashion at the time. As I mentioned, we had to exchange about $100 of US Currency for Levs and Stotinkis when we crossed the border, however, no one would accept the currency in Sofia. Everyone wanted either US Dollars or your American Express card; sorry Visa and Master Card were not accepted in Bulgaria back then. Anyone with an American Express card was a God as it was accepted everywhere, got you out of traffic tickets and got you into the better restaurants even if you didn't have a reservation. The same was true at our hotel where we were given the best available room because we were using American Express. What I remember most about Sofia, other than the truly bad food they served there, was the radio in our hotel room. This baby had to be at least 3' long and about a foot high and wide. Plus, it only got one radio station. Sorry no TVs in hotel rooms back then. Anyway, my wife and I were convinced that the Bulgarians had either put a bug in this radio or better yet, a midget was actually in the radio recording whatever we said or did while in the room. As a result, there was no sex on the nights we spent in Sofia, as my wife didn't want this recorded by some strangers. I was a bit paranoid about listening devices during the visit, as I knew that our Embassy there had recently found several devices in their walls.

So after two fun years at the Consulate General in Istanbul I received orders to report to The Hague, the Netherlands, after taking some Home Leave back in the USA.

OFF TO THE LAND OF WINDMILLS, WOODEN SHOES & TULIPS

Before our arrival in The Hague, around 1976 or so, the incidence of terrorism began to rise throughout the world and Embassies began to address the problem. Before then we had our anti-American demonstrations, an occasional crank or an isolated incidence of violence against the United States but nothing on a major scale. Just before going to The Hague the Japanese Red Army (JRA) attacked and took over the French Embassy in The Hague. The Ambassador and ten other people were taken hostage and a Dutch policewoman was shot. The hostages were eventually freed in exchange for the release of a jailed Red Army member, $300,000 and the use of a plane. The plane flew the hostage-takers first to Aden, South Yemen, where they were not accepted. They finally ended up in Syria. Syria did not consider hostage taking for money revolutionary, and the government forced them to give up their ransom. Then in 1979, just after I had departed this assignment, the British Ambassador was assassinated as he left his home on the way to the British Embassy. Although the IRA was suspected at the time for the assassination, this was never proved until a few years later.

During my assignment to The Hague two terrorist incidents took place in northern Holland that were carried out by the Moluccans, who were of Indonesian decent and had arrived in the Netherlands for a temporary stay and had been promised that they would get their own independent state, the Republik Maluku Selatan. For about 25 years they lived in temporary camps, often in poor conditions. As the years passed by the younger generation began to become more radical in order to gain some attention for their cause. In May 1977, two separate incidents took place that captured the attention of the world. On the morning of Monday, May 23, 1977, four armed South-Moluccans took over a school with 105 children and their five teachers in the Dutch province of Drenthe. At the same time, nine others hijacked a train in nearby De Punt and took 50 people hostage. Both incidents lasted about 20 days and ended when Royal Dutch Marines, acting under cover of darkness were able to determine the location of the hijackers on the train and later unleashed a barrage of bullets, later estimated at 15,000 rounds, at selected cars of the train killing the hijackers and two hostages. When the hostage takers at the school heard the news of their comrades, they surrendered just as the Royal Dutch Marines carried out their attack on the schoolhouse. I later saw photos of the train following the assault and many of the cars and the locomotive looked like swiss cheese with thousands of holes through them. The school incident was particularly interesting as this was the first time that I could remember terrorists taking over a school with small children in it. Before this incident schools were normally off limits to terrorists because of the possible bad publicity they might receive if small children are involved. Unfortunately attacks on schools both outside the US and within the US are now everyday news.

These were some of the highlights of the major terrorist activity during my two years in The Hague although we did have a few minor incidents take place during my tour there. One that sticks in my mind and is a bit laughable because of when it happened. I should mention here that the US Embassy in The Hague was right on the street and it was before the time that we concerned ourselves with putting up barriers or closing streets in front of our diplomatic facilities for fear of a terrorist attack. One night while the Marine Security Guard sat at his desk, which was several feet back from the front door and enclosed with bullet proof glass, an individual stopped his car right in front of the main entrance, left his vehicle carrying a tire iron and tried to break through the bullet proof doors at the main entrance. The Marine stood there in total amazement and sounded an emergency alarm to police headquarters while the intruder continued to beat on the doors. After realizing that he was not going to be successful, the person walked back to his car and drove off. What makes this incident interesting was that it was at the height of a full moon and as I mentioned earlier in my book, nuts seemed to be affected and came out during full moons. This is not a theory but a well-documented fact if you examine history.

Our assignment in The Netherlands was an enjoyable one and the country is filled with all sorts of museums to visit, bike trails that allow you to peddle to any of the adjoining countries and being near to the rest of Europe for fairly easily travel and touring. The beach is in the northern part of the city and beaches stretch along the coast of the North Sea. There is also an abundance of public parks throughout The Hague and other Dutch cities and weekends are spent by everyone walking in the parks and taking in nature while enjoying an ice cream or frites, the Dutch name for French fries. Frites came in a variety of configurations. You could get them plain, with mayonnaise or with Pindasaus, which was a peanut type sauce. When we first arrived in Holland and heard about these varieties we thought it was gross to eat French fries with mayo or peanut sauce but later came to love both versions. Dutch food as a whole wasn't anything to write home about. The most famous item Dutch food was a large pancake called a Pannekoeken, which besides putting syrup on it could have meat or cheese on it and measured about a foot across. You needed a special Pannekoeken plate to eat one. Most of the other Dutch dishes were of the meat and potato type and nothing very special. What was good food in Holland was the wide array of Indonesian food throughout the country. Rijsttafel was very popular at some of the restaurants and was a sort of Indonesian buffet or rice table. Also very good and very popular was going to Amsterdam and visiting the China Town there and getting their famous dim sim for breakfast or an early lunch.

The Dutch are also famous for their beers, Heineken and Grolsch in particular, and their Bols liqueurs. One of the most popular tourist stops was the Heineken Brewery in Amsterdam, especially by the college age crowds. It wasn't that most people were interested in how Heineken beer was actually brewed but rather the fact that at the conclusion of the tour you could sit in the beer hall and drink to your hearts content and snack on some food bits that were also set out. Many of the kids would do one tour, go back outside and get in line for a second or perhaps even a third tour. By the time they finished their tours and beer hall treats they were pretty much three sheets to the wind and only had to pay a minimal tour fee to get drunk.

As I said, there was an endless network of bike trails throughout Holland and you could bike through Holland and to a number of the adjoining countries without ever getting on or crossing a major highway. Restaurants and Inn stops were located along the routes so that you could spend several days biking through the country and stop for the night when you wanted. The Dutch as a whole were a very active people and most biked to work rather than driving. Furthermore, bicycles had the right of way on roadways and autos had to yield to them under penalty of heavy fines. I got into that habit early in my tour there and found I could usually bike to work or someplace I needed to go a lot easier than driving my car or taking public transportation. Dutch public transportation was fantastic however, and both the trains and buses were radio controlled and usually left at the exact minute that they were scheduled to either arrive or depart. You just bought a ticket for the bus or train and took off on your trip. It was in part on the honor system as tickets weren't checked while boarding, however, there were inspectors who routinely traveled the bus routes and boarded buses at random locations and inspected your ticket, both to see that you had one and secondly to see that you punched in upon boarding the bus. Penalty for failure to do either was an immediate fine on the spot while having everyone on the bus look at you in disgust for being dishonest.

Train travel throughout Europe was well ahead of our transportation system in the United States and you could travel quickly and fairly inexpensively almost anywhere. We made several trips to Brussels, Belgium, by train, as it was easier and quicker than driving. One trip in particular was pretty funny. Pat and I boarded the train and found our assigned train car and got seated. A few minutes before we left the station an old man, slightly in disarray, entered our train car with a carry bag of what appeared to be his belongings, a number of newspapers and some food. After the train got going this gentleman decided to clean and rearrange his bag while sitting across from us. He began to take objects out of the bag and at the same time crumbs of food began to fall out in front of him. As he continued to pull out newspapers, increasing amounts of crumbs and bits of food continued to fall out around him and towards us. Pat and I sat there smiling and trying to contain laughing out loud while this process continued unabated. Finally after about half an hour of this cleaning process, the man had refolded all his papers and belongings and decided to empty the bag out before repacking. He opened up the window in the train car and shook out his bag as all the crumbs and food bits started to fly throughout our train car. At this point Pat and I decided to evacuate our train car, assigned seats or not and burst out laughing while searching for a new car.

For God and Country

Speaking of assigned seats, like on the train, the Dutch were famous for assigning you to seats everywhere you went. We found out on our first venture to a Dutch Movie Theater that here too you were given an assigned seat. It made no difference that there were only four people in the entire theater or that all four of you were sitting right next to each other. You were assigned a seat and God help you if you decided to move. Case in point. Pat and I go to a movie. Five people in their assigned seats, next to each other, while the rest of the theater was entirely empty. Pat decides she is going to seat somewhere else. All of a sudden a woman usher comes up to her to see what she could ever be doing. Pat responds that she has changed her seat as the theater is almost empty and she didn't like her assigned seat. Wrong answer! The usher tells Pat to get back in her seat as other people may arrive later and be assigned to the seat she is now in. Also the penalty for failure to obey an usher, immediate expulsion from the theater. So the five of us sat, shoulder to shoulder, for the remainder of the movie.

Another thing the Dutch had way before the United States were cameras at many of the traffic lights in town and camera coverage on highways to catch speeders. You knew you had run a red light if you drove through an intersection and saw a bright flash. Same was true along major highways. If you were speeding and saw a flash from the side of the road, you knew you had been caught. Within a few days of the violation you received a traffic ticket in the mail complete with a photo of you running the red light, or if it was a speeding violation, a photo of your car on the highway along with the speed you were doing underneath the photo. One of the biggest violators of red lights was our Ambassador. He had a small sports car although I can't recall the make. We continually received photos at the Security Office of the Ambassador with the top down, a big smile on his face and a photo of the red light. The Ambassador had decreed that diplomatic immunity or not, we were responsible for paying for all traffic violations, so we sent all his violations to his office for his payment.

The other cool thing about the Dutch was the Dutch State Police or Rijkspolitie. These guys drove Porsche 911 Targus, and in the winter months they drove with the top off, while wearing white leather, fur trimmed coats, leather tanker's hats and goggles. You'd be driving along the major highways and have these guys blow by you at a 100 mph with the wind blowing in their faces and a big smile. The other peculiar roadway regulation in Holland was that all traffic yielded to the right. So any time you came to an intersection you had to yield to cars coming from your right even if you were on the main thoroughfare. This took a little getting used to, to say the least.

As I mentioned, there were beaches all along the North Sea and even if the water temperatures left a little to be desired during the summer, people still went to the beach and swam. We had heard numerous stories about the famous or infamous Nude Beach somewhere along the North side of The Hague. Since Pat and I frequently walked or biked along this area we were constantly on the lookout for this famous beach, mainly out of curiosity and because we thought this was an urban legend. Then one day, low and behold, we finally find the beach and wished we hadn't. No young women or guys here. No sir, folks in their 50's and 60's, completely nude, and not the sight you wanted to see at any time.

Speaking of nudity, Amsterdam was famous for its Red Light district with hookers sitting in windows and all sorts of sex shows and shops along Canal Street. Our Dutch language instructor told us that Holland was famous all over the world for its Red Light District and sex shows and that many transvestites would board planes in London as men and got off in Amsterdam dressed as women. During my parent's visit to Holland, my father particularly liked walking along here and taking photos of everything he saw, much to our embarrassment. There was a similar area in The Hague but it was only a block square. Whenever we went out with my parents, they somehow always directed us to drove around these blocks for their amusement. As I remember, if you started at side one of the block the women were fairly pretty but as you continued around the block the level of beauty quickly diminished. One night there was even a dog sitting in one of the windows on a chair. We weren't sure if his mistress had taken a break or if that's who was in the little room behind the window. The women sat in large windows for your viewing and selection and behind them was a curtain and a small 6'X6" room with a sink and a bed where the dirty deeds took place. Prostitution is regulated by the Dutch Government and women were regularly checked by doctors so that the trade keep fairly clean and healthy. It was major employment for many single and married women and I understand the pay wasn't too bad.

There was also a wide array of sex shops throughout most cities in Holland that sold a variety of sex toys and various objects. One shop near a movie theater we frequented had a leopard skin looking object that neither my wife nor I could figure out but was nonetheless interesting to checkout in the window whenever we went by. There was also a small pair of latex rubber gloves in the window, about the size that you fit a doll, which completely baffled us as well as to their use.

One funny story I remember involved the Halloween Party that the Marines held at the Marine House. Everyone got dressed up to go to the party although Halloween wasn't widely celebrated in Holland at the time. Pat and I decide to go to the party with some friends from the Defense Attaché's Office (DATT). Pat dressed as a nun and my friend's wife dressed as a pirate, complete with a long black mustache and pirate's hat. My friend dressed up like a mummy with bandages over his body and face and so you couldn't tell who he could possibly be. Likewise my costume is a great disguise as I combed out our Afghan Hound and took all his hair and glued it on my face with theatrical glue and then put in a set of fangs and painted my nose black so I looked like a werewolf. My friend and I decided that our identity's would be given away if we entered the party with our wife's so we tell them to drop us off and then park by the house and wait about 10 minutes before coming in. The women followed our instructions and are sitting in the car after they dropped us off, a nun and a pirate, side by side. The Dutch Police are patrolling the house as it is the American Embassy's Marine House and so after three passes of our vehicle they decide that there is something strange about these two people sitting there for over 10 minutes. Maybe they might be terrorists or something.

They stop their police car, get out of the car and knock on the window, and the pirate lowers the window while the nun looks on. Fortunately they knew what Halloween was and after a little explanation by our wives decide not to arrest Pat and her sidekick. Our wives later come into the Marine House and tell us the whole story but up until this point our identities are still a mystery to all in attendance at the party. Mission accomplished, although the wives were a little pissed.

The movie theaters in The Hague were all modern and usually got all the newest American movies, sometimes even before they hit theaters in the US. As I mentioned before, you bought your ticket and were assigned a seat and God help you if you moved from that seat, as you would get the wraith of the usher or usherette. One other thing I failed to mention about the movies in Holland. You could buy yourself a Heineken beer before you went into the theater and smoking at the time was permitted in the theater too. So there you sat as your neighbors in the theater puffed away on their cigarettes and drank beer, many of whom were Dutch youth. Dutch youth have a history of being a bit unruly until they reach a certain age in life, what that was I'm not sure. Anyway, it was not uncommon for kids to flip their lit cigarette butts at the movie screen or if they didn't like a certain scene or the action in the movie, throw their empty or sometimes full beer bottles at the screen. We found out early on from friends that you always attempted to sit under the balcony section in the movie theater least someone drop their beer bottle on your head from above.

We also found out that holidays in Holland and certain countries of Europe were celebrated much differently from how we did things in the US. Christmas in Holland was a big holiday like it is in America and stores were filled with all kind of taste treats, candies and holiday cakes and cookies. We usually sent some of these back home on the holidays as they weren't available back home and this was way before people could buy just about anything on the Internet. The major difference between Christmas in the US and Holland was a character named Black Pete. He is the companion of Saint Nicholas but concentrates only on all the bad boys and girls and brings them coal if they've been bad. Everyone decorated like in the states and streets and stores were lavishly decorated for the holidays. Most Dutch holidays, however, were reserved for the family and not usually celebrated with outsiders. Case in point. We invited the Senior Police Inspector and his assistant along with their wife's over for Thanksgiving dinner as we thought they might like to see how Americans celebrated that holiday. Pat prepared the traditional turkey dinner with all the trimmings and when the group arrived we had a few drinks before sitting down to the big meal. The row home we lived in was small, as was our dining room, so we decided that a buffet would work best for getting everyone fed. We set up the food on a side table and Pat and I led the way in the food line. Everyone got up except the Sr. Inspector's spouse who just sat there, unmoving, while everyone else filled their plates with Thanksgiving treats. I finally decided to ask her why she wasn't getting any food and her response startled me. She said, "We had to stand in line during the war to get our food and I won't stand in line now to get mine!" OK! So maybe you want me or your husband to fix you a plate? I think she did eventually eat but I am not sure how her food got from point A to point B.

I'll talk about our New Year's experience before I get back to the Dutch and their deep dislike of the Germans, many years after the war. New Years was a different experience too for Pat and I in Holland. We were used to going out and living it up and maybe even getting a good drunk with our friends. New Year's Eve came along and we decided to go out with some friends and get dinner and hit some bars before the New Year arrived. Wrong! Nothing was open and I mean nothing. The town was deserted. We went back home to try to figure out what to do. Seems that New Years was a very family type holiday and everyone went to their family's homes for dinner, drinking etc., and there were no ball dropping celebrations in The Hague that we could find. About 5 minutes before midnight you would have thought that WW III had broken out, as there were fireworks and explosions all over the town, which lasted from about five minutes before until five minutes after twelve midnight. Then it was total silence once again. That was New Years as we celebrated back in the 70's in Holland. I'm sure it's a lot different now.

Now I'll get back to the Dutch and their dislike of the Germans. There is no love lost between the Dutch and the Germans and the Dutch still remember WW II vividly. All around the City of The Hague are reminders of the war. Throughout the many parks in the city sit concrete bunkers that are only visible to the casual passerby during the winter months when all the leaves had fallen. The Atlantic Wall, a coastal defense built by the Germans to the north of the city, still remains with its

71

large concrete bunkers where German guns once protected this avenue to the Netherlands. During the war the Dutch were required to keep their drapes closed at night to prevent light from escaping their homes. After the war, and when we lived in The Hague, city dwellers all kept their drapes wide open at night in defiance of what had been levied upon them during the war. Pat and I followed the Dutch tradition and left our drapes open at night just as the Dutch did. It was funny however when we watched television at night because people walking along the street would regularly stop and join us in watching a TV program while they stood outside and looked into our living room. Us on our couch in the living room and they on the sidewalk outside. The Germans also initiated daylight savings during the war and until the 1970's, when we resided there, the Dutch would not go onto daylight savings time because it was originally a German thing. God forbid that you attempted to speak Dutch and pronounced the word like the Germans did. The Dutch were quick to reprimand you and advise you that what you just said was the German pronunciation and not the Dutch version. Learning Dutch was a very frustrating venture. Pat and I took lessons every week and made attempts to learn and speak the language but it was a lost endeavor. Unless you spoke Dutch perfectly, the person you were speaking to in your Dutch would usually repeat what you had attempted to say in English and then answer you in English. After a while we just gave up as most people in the major cities spoke English anyway. In fact, most Dutch children spoke three or four languages by the time they finished their schooling.

For God and Country

In the springtime it was fun to drive through the countryside and look at the many varieties of tulips that grew throughout Holland. Even the local parks had tulip beds throughout them. I always thought that there were only 2-4 kinds of tulips but quickly found out that there were hundreds of varieties and colors of the flower that made Holland famous. Then there were the many varieties of windmills throughout the countryside, the many canals and of course the many types of cheese the country produced. The northern parts of Holland were famous for their cheeses and had contests, mostly for the tourists, where they raced between two points carrying and weighing cheeses on wooden sleds. We were lucky during our tour in The Netherlands as the canals froze over for the first time in many years, allowing people to go skating on the canals. This didn't happen every year and I think it had been about 10 years since they had frozen last.

If you believe in reincarnation and the possibility that you could be reborn as someone else or perhaps an animal, say a dog, then Holland is the place you want to be reborn in. We traveled throughout Holland and most of Europe while assigned to The Hague and Europeans as a whole love animals and especially dogs. We got into a number of hotels while traveling with our Afghan Hound when people in line ahead of us with children were told there was no room. In Holland you could take your dog just about everywhere. I think the only place dogs weren't allowed was the butcher shop. On buses we bought Boris a children's ticket and if there were seats available he could flop his ass on the bus seat and sit there. A number of times he would end up next to some old woman who would hold and hug him while we headed to our destination. At restaurants he was free to sit next to the table and to partake in the meal if we decided to feed him. Hell, I even saw dogs sitting on chairs right at the table just like the people they belonged to. Same was true of shops and even department stores. The only trick with the latter was teaching Boris how to ride the escalator if we wanted to go to the second floor. Dogs were everywhere in Holland and there was only one rule you had to obey. Don't let your dog shit on the sidewalk. There were even signs stenciled on the sidewalks telling people that. In looking at the Internet recently I see that it has gotten so bad with dog shit everywhere that the Dutch have initiated stiff fines for violators. As we all know, there's nothing like stepping on dog shit while you outside walking.

One final humorous story before we depart The Hague. Stephen King had published his book "Salem's Lot" while we were in The Hague. As far as King's books go this was perhaps one of his best and definitely one of the scariest ones for reading late at night in your house alone. Several of the secretaries at the Embassy decided to read the book and some got so scared reading it alone in their homes at night that they would only read it at work. So you would see them throughout the day reading the book in the daylight and at their desks. A few even became so obsessed and scared reading the book that they took up wearing crucifixes around their necks both at work and at home, least they encounter a vampire somewhere. One of our close friends, Faye, found an old cross and began to wear it 24 hours a day for fear that a vampire might otherwise get her. One night, when Pat's brother and his wife were visiting us, we were invited to Faye's house for dinner. We had told Pat's brother about Faye and why she was wearing the cross. When we arrived at the house and rang the doorbell, Faye answered the door and let everyone in. Pat's brother lagged behind and didn't enter, however. Faye asked him what was wrong and he replied, " That she had to invite him in." So Faye said, "Come in please." Whereupon Pat's brother replied in his best Dracula voice, "Thank you very much." The joke being that vampires couldn't enter someone's house without first being invited inside. The result was laughter from everyone in the house.

So after about two years into my assignment I came back to the Embassy after having lunch with some security rep and have my assignment cable waiting for me. The cable says, " Congratulations you have been assigned as the Regional Security Officer to New Delhi, India, per your bid cable." I think for a minute before I open my safe and get my bid cable out. (RSOs have to submit at least six bids when their tour, at that time 2 years, is almost ready to end) I scan my cable carefully and No Where do I see that I had ever bid, or for that matter thought about, bidding on New Delhi, India. So New Delhi, India is where Pat and I are off to for my next assignment with DS. When I got home and give Pat the news, she is sure that I was taking her from a nice posting like The Hague to the other end of the world and possibly HELL. After finally convincing Pat that New Delhi must have some positive aspects to it she finally resigns herself to life in Delhi for 2 years. A few days later my career counselor called me and told me he had great news. I was being considered for either Moscow or

Tehran, Iran, in lieu of Delhi. I politely tell him to forget it. My wife is now OK with Delhi and so lets leave it at that and he agreed to do so. As a quick note. Had I been paneled for and given Tehran as my next assignment I would have had the pleasure of spending about 444 days as a hostage there as this was the same timeframe that the Embassy in Tehran was taken over by Iranian students and most of our employees taken hostage.

So sometime around the end of June Pat and I board the old Pan Am One Flight that flies around the world and depart for New Delhi, India. Good Bye Holland!

INDIA-LAND OF HUNDUISM & 1.2 BILLION PEOPLE

When we departed The Hague at the end of June 1978 we were still wearing our winter coats when we boarded Pan Am One. We had packed all our household items, including our winter clothes, as we didn't think we'd need them in India. Little did we know that it would be a long winter in Holland and that we'd have to go out and buy more coats so we wouldn't freeze before we left. The Pan Am around the world flight arrived in New Delhi about 3 a.m. and the plane parked a fair distance from the terminal so that we had to depart the plane via the stairs they rolled over to the plane and walk to the terminal. As we neared the bottom of the stairs all we could see on the ground were thousands and thousands of bugs crawling all over the tarmac of the airport. We would later learn that the locusts were swarming and landing all over the city. We walked to the terminal, crunching locust after locust with each step. Pat looked at me with this look that almost said, "Where the Fuck have you taken me?" We finally got to the terminal and waited for our baggage and our Afghan Hound Boris to arrive in his Livingston Cattle Company cage. The bags and our dog arrived and we took Boris out of his cage and started off to Immigration and Customs counters. It is like Moses parting the Red Sea. The Indians jumped out of the way as Boris led the way for us. Most feared that he would either bite them, eat them or definitely give them rabies as the Indians weren't big dog lovers. We made it to Customs before everyone else on the flight since they didn't have Boris breaking a path for them. We present our dog's vaccination certificate to the customs agent who barely looks at it. He does however ask how much the dog is worth. I ask him what he wants to know. He says" Is your dog worth more or less than $100." I reply that Boris is worth much more than $100 and he then tells me that I have to pay a duty to bring him into the country. I quickly retort that Boris is a very old dog and so even though I paid more than $100 when I bought him, he has depreciated over the years and now would be worth much less than $100. This seems to satisfy the customs man as he agrees with what I have told him and stamps our papers for entry into India. Problem resolved.

We depart the airport with the embassy meet and greet people and head directly to our new home, which comes complete with our very own cook and house boy, Peter and Savone. Our name is even already painted on the plaque at the front of the house and we are ready to move right in. New Delhi would turn our to be one of our most interesting posts both from a work standpoint and as far as traveling throughout the country and seeing India and its people. I was the Regional

Security Officer and covered not only India but also Nepal and Sri Lanka and so we got to see some different countries and a lot of unusual sights over the years we were assigned there. What was to be a two-year assignment turned out to be three years but I'll tell you about that later.

India took a little adjustment after having served in Holland and Turkey prior to this. Lepers on the street corners begging whenever you stopped for a traffic light, beggars throughout the city, people squatting in fields and doing their business, cows and other animals walking across or along roadways, in addition to monkeys, peacocks and naked holy men.

India has the caste system of society and if you are born into a certain caste, that is where you remain for the rest of your life, no matter what education or training you may gain throughout your life. Parents would maim their children so that they could beg on street corners and become legitimate beggars for the rest of their lives. The embassy doctor advised us shortly after arriving that the dirt and dust blowing around New Delhi and throughout India was in fact human and animal fecal matter that had dried up and became powder. A great thing to think about as you walked around on a windy day.

Our household shipment finally arrived in Delhi after we had been there about 2 months and on the day of delivery we got a call at about 8 a.m. saying the container with our stuff had just left the warehouse and was on its way. I should add that the warehouse was perhaps 2 miles from our house. 9 a.m. came and went. Ten a.m. came and went. Eleven a.m. came and went.

79

Noon came and went. Time to call the embassy and see what happened. Was our stuff really on the way? Had it been hijacked and stolen? Was the vehicle in an accident? The response, "Soon to come!" Finally at 1 p.m. a wooden cart drawn by two oxen finally arrived at the house and there was our lift van with all our belongings sitting on top of a flat wooden cart. Service with a smile.

The Embassy had a wide array of facilities to take care of its employees during their tours. There was a fully equipped hospital in the basement of the Annex Building, complete with a sterile operating room and a baby nursery. Most of the equipment had come from the military after our withdrawal from Viet Nam. It was said that the operating room was one of the few fully sterile ORs in all of India at the time, although now India is famous for its luxury hospitals catering to foreigners and doing low budget operations for all kinds of major ailments. We had a full, 100+ seat, movie theater in the annex basement, complete with a ticket sales booth and hot popcorn sold by the bag. Movies were shown seven days a week in the evenings and we usually got some of the more current movies courtesy of the U.S. military. There were three Brunswick Bowling Alleys on the corner of the housing compound. Reportedly the only ones of their kind in all of India at the time. Bowling leagues ran nearly every night and the lanes had a complete snack bar serving those famous Indian beers with names like Rosy Pelican, Three Coins and King Fisher along with your U.S. favorites. We had a full restaurant that served decent lunches and dinners, pepper steak and cheeseburgers being my favorite. Some of our meats came from Australia; however, most of the ingredients were bought locally. We really didn't have real steak or beef in India as the cow was a sacred animal and was never killed for food. Instead we had wonderful water buffalo steaks, which, if they marinade long enough in some kind of sauce, were edible and we finally got used to eating. There was the Marine House that had weekly TGIFs and usually drew a large crowd from the diplomatic community along with some Indian girlfriends of the Marines. We had three tennis courts and two Indian professional instructors who taught you whatever stroke you wanted to do on a particular day. There were also balls boys at the courts so you didn't have to shag the balls yourself. We had a full super market that had some U.S. items plus items from Australia and neighboring countries. Lastly, we had a full baseball field complete with an outfield scoreboard and some little kid keeping score by hanging numbers on hooks. There was also a popcorn and hotdog guy who walked among the bleachers and sold these items along with sodas and beer during the games. The embassy had several baseball teams from among the 350+ Americans assigned there. Once a year the embassy sponsored a world series of baseball with Indian teams coming from throughout the country to play against the Americans. We even had games under the lights, as the stadium was fully equipped for night games. The amount of electricity used during one night game probably equaled the amount of electricity used by the entire city. Hey, the Americans always do it big. The World Series drew teams from all over the country and the ballgames ran continuously for almost a full week with the victor being crowned at the end.

Pat and I did a lot of reading while we were assigned to Delhi, as there was virtually no worthwhile television to watch. We had a black and white TV from Holland and the only two English-speaking programs on local TV were the Indian farm report and "I Love Lucy." That was it. It was also before computers and Netflix and VCRs were just starting to come out and sold for close to a thousand dollars at the time. There were always numerous dinner parties, regular parties and embassy events for entertainment. It was so cheap to do a party that nearly every weekend someone was having one. The average cost for a party for close to a hundred people with food, entertainment and local decorations was maybe $100-$200. One year we decided to have a Halloween Party at our house and with the help of my local staff ended up throwing one of the parties of the year. We have a large tent constructed completely over and around the house. For entertainment we hired a few local entertainers, a magician and fortuneteller and we decided that we wanted a marching band staged in the driveway and playing as the guests arrived. This was before there were any good rock bands in Delhi so my local assistant said he could get the Police band to play and it would only cost about $25 and plus a case of American beer. I said "Sure." The night of the party a bus pulled up to the house and out came the entire Police Band, all 30 or so members, complete with a real drum major. Needless to say this attracted the attention from our Indian neighbors especially once the band cranked up the music and the march tunes. Neighbors piled out of their houses along the street to see what those crazy Americans could possibly be doing. Then the guests began to arrive and that brought out the rest of the neighbors to see what was happening at our house. Superman, Indian dressed men and women, Afghan dressed people and so many different types of getups that I can't remember. Food, booze and dancing continued into the wee hours of the morning as the neighbors stood along the street taking in the sites, keeping tune to the music and maybe doing a little dancing in the streets themselves.

The other great party that took place annually was New Year's Eve Party hosted by the communications section at the embassy. Guests were told to arrive early and park in a large lot between the embassy and the party site. After waiting a few minutes a wooden cart, drawn by 2 oxen (maybe the same ones that delivered our household stuff) arrived and we were told to take a seat in the back of the cart. An audiotape was then played advising us that we were on Ox Cart Number 1 and would be departing shortly to our destination. Off we went for a 1/2 mile road trip and finally arrived at the party house complete with an Indian tent all around it and music going strong from inside. Plenty of eating and drinking and at midnight, both Father Time and Baby New Year arrived in full party dress. Turns out that Baby New Year was the junior Special Agent in my office and as the night went on and people got drunk, the ladies in the crowd tried to pull off the large diaper he was wearing.

Although I don't remember much about Christmas in New Delhi I do remember a fairly funny story that took place around Christmas time the first year we were there. You have to remember that this was way before the iPhone and cell phones that let you call anywhere in the world without the assistance of an operator. Back in the 80's in India we had to book our calls back home well in advance of when we actually wanted to make a call. So people booked their Christmas calls back to home about a week before hand and sometime on Christmas Day the phone would ring and you hopefully had your party on the line. During everyone's arrival briefing at the Security Office we warned people to watch what they said on the phone since we thought the Indians were probably listening in on everyone's phone calls. Most people shock their heads in acknowledgement but probably thought we had been watching too many James Bond movies. This was India and most things didn't work well or were antiquated, so how could the Indians possibly be listening in. So one officer decides to place a call to his daughter in the U.S. over the Christmas holidays and then has a nice conversation with her when the call comes through on Christmas Day. About a week later, this same officer's phone rings at his home in Delhi and when he lifts up the receiver he hears the entire conversation that he had the week before with his daughter. The next workday he comes running into the security office to tell us his tale and to inform us that maybe the Indian Government is listening in to our telephone conversations. Dah! Didn't you go to our security briefing when you arrived in India and didn't we tell you that this might happen?

We had local guards called chaukeedaars at our homes during the evening and night hours as house break-ins did occur in Delhi on a regular basis. At night the guard walked around the house and hit the stick he carried, a laathi, on the sides of the house so the occupants would know he was awake and doing his job.

This was fine, however, he tended to concentrate on the bedroom area during his rounds as he knew the saahab (master/boss) and his wife were inside and would hear this noise from his vigil. What he didn't realize was that it also kept us up or wake us up if he hit the stick too hard against the house. Guards were forever falling asleep both at the Embassy and at people's homes. One night we returned home fairly late to find our guard sound asleep in a chair outside the vehicle gate, with his chair propped solidly against it. After blowing my car horn unsuccessfully several times to wake him, Pat exited the car and kicked the chair out from under him and this barely woke him from his sound sleep. Another time my assistant at the security office had the government car at home, which was equipped with police lights and a siren. Upon driving into his driveway he found the guard sound asleep and lying in the driveway. He drove the car over top of the guard and hit the siren. This did wake the guard up but also produced a slight headache when he banged his head on the bottom the car. Guards were on the bottom of the totem pole as far as the caste system went. They did do a good job as a whole and sometimes were beaten or badly injured when robbers tried to break into homes and attacked them. India had several noted robbers throughout the country but the most famous robber in the 80's was Phoolan Devi, also known as the Bandit Queen. Some people saw her violence as the lower castes' retaliation against the cruelty of the upper-castes. In 1983, she finally surrendered to police officials after several years of lawlessness and was tried for complicity in over 30 instances of murder and numerous other crimes. She spent 11 years in prison while her trial was pending. She was further made famous when a movie was made of her life in 1994 and in 2001 she was shot and killed by unknown assailants. India wasn't the Wild West but certain areas of the country were pretty dangerous to travel in.

I had a number of major security incidents while assigned to Delhi, some of which were funny to think about in later years and others very sad. One night I was sitting at home reading when I received a phone call from the Marine Security Guard at the Embassy who advised me that there was fire at the Annex Building. When I asked him to describe how bad the fire was, he responded, "I think the word they would use is raging out of control." That gave me a pretty clear picture of what to expect when I finally got to the embassy. Upon arriving I could see smoke and flames shooting out some windows in the Annex Building and when I got to the lobby and tried to enter so I could evaluate things the smoke was so thick that I have to abandon the idea. Finally the Delhi Fire Department arrived in what I would estimate was a 1940s or so fire truck and a hand full of men. I tell the Fire Chief that the building is filled with smoke and it will be difficult for his men to enter, as they have no breathing apparatus with them. He assures me that they are used to entering burning and smoke filled buildings and proceeds to enter the building to access the situation. About thirty-seconds later he comes out of the building coughing and tells me that he doesn't think they can enter the building as they have no breathing apparatus. We finally decide to attack the fire from the outside and his men begin to break out windows on the second floor of the Annex and pour water from their truck into the building. We had planned to tie his hoses into the standpipes of the embassy's fire system but found out quickly that the pipes were bone dry and haven't been tested in several years. After several hours and lots and lots of water, I manage to get into the building with some of the Marines to assess the building and the damage. There were still a few small fires that we put out with portable extinguishers and fire damage was limited to about 6 offices but there was extreme water damage on several floors. Water had run from the top floor to the first floor and down into the basement level. Water was everywhere and it would take quite a bit of pumping to eventually get all the water out of the building. Our investigation of the fire begins with the General Services Officer and myself walking through the second floor of the Annex and we quickly determine the cause of the fire based on the concentrated burn in one office. It seems that someone had been making something on a hotplate when the power at the embassy went off. The power stayed off for several hours and eventually the local employees put their things away and went home at 5:00 P.M. This included the still plugged in hotplate that was put away in a cabinet by someone. When the power eventually came back on several hours later, it started a fire in the cabinet that spread through the office and then traveled to some other offices through the air conditioning ducts. Damage was several thousands dollars but the annex was partially up and running by the next workday although there still was the heavy scent of smoke in the building for a few weeks.

Another evening I received a call from the Marine Security Guard telling me that one of the communicators, who owned a pink Cadillac convertible, had somehow landed his car smack dab in the middle of one the fountains on the street in front of the embassy. I drive down to the embassy and sure enough there is a big old pink Cadillac sitting in the middle of the fountain and a very drunk communicator close by. When I ask the Embassy guards what happened they described the incident as follows. The car was driving down the main street toward the Embassy's main vehicle entrance and the closer the car got to the Embassy, the faster it went, until, while traveling at a very high rate of speed it hit the curb in front of the fountain, became airborne and landed right in the middle of the fountain. Definitely a sight to behold. Too bad I didn't think to get a picture. The story doesn't end here however. Employees are allowed the import of only one vehicle into India per tour. The communicator's car was pretty much totaled and he couldn't fix the car nor could he buy a second vehicle as he was allowed the import of only into the country. The pink Cadillac sat for about 2 years in back of the housing compound, a monument to what one can do when they're drinking and driving. Finally the employee's assignment is over and he is ready to depart India. The employee has to either sell this car or take it with him when he departs post according to Indian Government Regulations for Embassy personnel. Since he can't sell the car the Indian government tells him he either has to take it with him or get rid of it somehow but he cannot do so in India. Fortunately there was a U.S. Government support flight arriving in Delhi to deliver materials to the Embassy and after some fast talking with the flight crew and the front office at the Embassy we manage to get the car put on the plane that it is scheduled to head back to the U.S. Stories have it that somewhere over the Indian Ocean, the back cargo door opened and the pink Cadillac dropped into the depths of the ocean, never to be seen again and where it is presumably still resting even today.

We had a large number of demonstrations in Delhi directed against our Embassy during my tour there. What was interesting however was that many of the demonstrations were organized by the communists and the demonstrators were usually paid to go out and demonstrate at a particular location which could be our Embassy or some other location. Not only were the demonstrators paid but the duration of the demonstration was always predetermined, usually by the amount of money the organizer was willing to pay out. On the scheduled day the demonstrators would show up in some sort of bus, pile out and do their shouting and yelling for X-number of minutes and then someone would check his watch and determine that they had done the agreed upon time demonstrating and the signal went out to head back to the buses. That led to a stampede as usually the buses were filled to the capacity and slow runners usually ended up either on the roof of the bus or walking back home.

Buses and trains were often filled to or beyond capacity and it was common to see scores of people on bus and train tops riding to their destinations. It was also common to read in the newspaper that someone was standing up and not paying attention when the train went through an overpass or tunnel and that several people were killed.

As I mentioned, cows and some other animals were considered sacred and if or when they decided to cross or sit in the middle of the highway, you better not hit them or else. One time a large reddish bull, who we fondly named Big Red, decided that it was time for a little break and he sat down in the middle of the road that I took daily to get to work. He remained there for about two weeks. The bull didn't appear to be injured and people brought him food daily along with buckets of water, so he was perfectly happy just sitting and staying where he was. Finally one day he wasn't there anymore as I drove into work. I'm not sure if he died or just decided it was time to move on.

Another time, I was coming home late from a TGIF at the Marine House when I vaguely see a group of something barreling down the road and aiming right at my car. I hit the brakes, only to see about fifteen pigs running past me and headed for destinations unknown. Another frequent sight was the wooden cart going down the road and being drawn by either a camel or oxen with the driver sound asleep atop the cart and headed for wherever his animals decide to take him.

Another incident that occurred at the Embassy one night was perhaps the saddest in my career with DS and while serving overseas. I received a call at about 8:00 P.M. from the Marine Security Guard at Post#1 who advised me that one of the Marines had shot himself and that he appeared to have committed suicide on the front steps of the Embassy Chancery. I jumped into my car and raced to the Embassy only to find out that the Marine had already been taken to a local hospital that was a short distance from the Embassy. All that remained at the scene was a puddle of blood and some skull fragments on the landing. It appeared that the Marine had sat on the landing in front of the Chancery and then shot himself with his service revolver. After the shots (there were in fact two shots discharged) were fired he somehow managed to key his radio which led the Marine at Post #1 to ascertain that something was wrong and he began a search for the second Marine who was on duty with him. The Marine finally found the wounded Marine and an ambulance took him to a nearby Indian Hospital. My investigation found and theorized that he was having some personal problems, perhaps with his girlfriend, and something just triggered him to take his own life. We later pieced together some additional details of that night but were never 100% sure what the exact reason was for this very popular Marine to take his own life. Several weeks after the incident our office became involved in a Congressional Inquiry regarding the young Marine's death as someone in his family believed that there were suspicious circumstances surrounding his death. The Inquiry even hinted that perhaps he had found out something that he shouldn't have and that the U.S. Government was responsible for killing him. This theory was quickly dispelled and proven to be completely false as there was never any evidence that this was anything other than an unfortunate suicide.

The Embassy in New Delhi was built by Edward Stone, who also built the Kennedy Center in Washington, D.C. Both buildings are very similar in design, as I understand Stone designed the Embassy in 1959 and then used that basic design for the Kennedy Center that was built a number of years later. The

Embassy compound consisted of the main Chancery, an annex building, the Ambassador's Residence and a large housing compound where a number of staff employees were housed along with the Embassy's recreation facilities and a Marine House. It was one of the largest embassies in the world at the time. Inside the Chancery was a large water pond with an open courtyard as the building was a large rectangle shape with an open roof over the pond. A plaque in front of the pond tells staff and visitors that this was the spot where former Ambassador Pickering fed his ducks and I believe some geese everyday. By the time I arrived in Delhi the ducks and geese had been removed from the water as they tended to jump out of the water and either chase employees as they came out of the offices surrounding the pond or enter the offices whenever they could. They also shit on the marble floors around the pond and gave several employees an exciting ride when they stepped on the wet marble and shit and went sliding along the walkway. The pond continually got dirty from smaller birds and dirt and dust landing in the water and so an official pond keeper had to be hired to keep the pond clean. The keeper would use a water vacuum and start vacuuming from one end of the large pond every Monday and finish his cleaning by Friday. By this time he was ready to start all over again the following Monday and so was guaranteed permanent employment by the embassy for as long as the pond remained.

Some American employees at the Embassy disliked India and many came there solely because it was a differential post because of the health hazards. This meant that most employees received as much a 25% more pay during their assignment. India was nonetheless an interesting and exciting place to live and travel through. Agra was perhaps the most famous tourist sight to visit and we traveled there on several occasions to see the beauty of the city and the famous Taj Mahal. We usually traveled throughout India by either plane or train as driving on roads outside the city was too much of an adventure and very dangerous because of the bad driving habits of the Indians and also the many animals one encountered onto the roadways. Trains could also be an adventure unless you booked first class seating as both people and animals traveled on the trains. They usually were overbooked and several people had to sit on top of the train cars for a ride to their final destination. Once you arrived at your destination you could catch a taxi, rickshaw or a "tuk-tuk", which is a three wheeled auto rickshaw and used throughout India for quick and very inexpensive travel. There were endless historic sites throughout India and most dated back centuries to the time of the sultans. There are also an abundance of holidays while living in India as the Embassy celebrated not only the American holidays but also the Indian and British holidays, since India had been under British rule at one time. There were numerous parades to celebrate various occasions and holidays but the biggest one held in Delhi was Republic Day which honored the date on which the Constitution of India came into force on 26 January 1950 and replaced the Government of India Act (1935) as the governing document of India. The diplomatic corps always received tickets for the prize seats to attend this event annually. The parade had numerous military units and floats in it and the camel corps and cavalry were a parade favorite. There are still parts of

India where vehicles, including 4 wheel drives, cannot maneuver and so camels and horses are still used by the Indian military to patrol these areas, especially along the borders of the country.

We were fortunate in that we could go horse back riding daily at the Polo Club, which was run, by the India Calvary and the President's Bodyguard. Lessons were given by a retired Indian Calvary Sergeant who taught us everything from the basics of horseback riding through advanced riding which entailed riding bareback, riding with and without stirrups, riding cross country and up and down the numerous hills at the riding club. We also learned how to jump over all kinds of obstacles including burning bundles of hay. This really sacred me as I was sure the horse would throw me off and into the burning pile. Fortunately most of the horses we rode were either retired military horses or polo ponies so they were used to this type of riding. We also took polo lessons and got a small taste of what it was like to play polo against each other. The instructor sergeant was an easygoing guy, however, if either you or your horse didn't follow instructions each of you would get a few quick hits from his riding crop to reinforce the lesson. One day I had a really bad experience while riding one of the larger horses at the club named Nelson. Nelson had a history of misbehaving and wasn't one of my favorites to ride. My favorite mount was an old Calvary horse who was shaped like a big barrel and named Mogul. He was easy going and well trained and followed your commands to the letter. Just the opposite of Nelson. One morning I mounted Nelson and start riding toward the riding ring for some formal type riding lessons. Half way to the ring

Nelson does a 180-degree turn and starts to race down the parade field. I pulled back on the reins and sat back in the saddle and tried to control and stop him but with little success. Instead, Nelson bites down on his bite and starts to accelerate even faster down the parade field and so I let him go a bit before I make another attempt to stop him. When I think he can't go any faster, he starts to accelerate even more until we are flying down the parade field faster than I thought a horse could run. Nelson does another 180 degree turn and heads toward the clubhouse and some unsuspecting gentleman sitting atop his horse. Nelson now adjusts his path and heads directly for the horse and his rider in almost a perfect line towards the center of the horse. At this point I thought to myself, "This horse can't be that stupid to hit this other horse and rider at a dead run." Wrong! We are now about 3 feet away when I realize that is just what he is going to do and so I hug Nelson around his neck and prepare for impact. Boom! We hit that other horse and both he and his rider go down to the ground. Nelson, however, continues down the field at a full gallop and I realize even more now that this horse is truly NUTS. I see another rider and yell for help as no matter how hard I pull on Nelson's reins or stand in my stirrups pulling at Nelson, he Does Not Slow down. The other rider suddenly rides in front of us and I manage slide off the back of Nelson as he slows bit but then continues to gallop away down the parade field, now rider less. I guess Nelson was finally caught by someone and brought back into the stables. By now the word had spread to all the people in my class and at the club that some rider and his crazy horse had just flattened some guy and his horse. My wife hears the news but had no idea that it is me everyone was talking about. Later when I talked to a few people who were having coffee at the club and watching this scene, they assured me that they had never seen a horse travel at the rate of speed that Nelson was doing that day.

Post Script: As this was the umpteen time that Nelson had done shit like that, the club decided that it was time to send him to that great stable in the sky and he was put down about a week later when he did a similar thing to a much less experienced lady rider at the club. When I hit the other horse my head was on the side of Nelson's head and I took a good shot to the head that resulted in a severe stiff neck, which didn't want to go away. We had a little old woman, Debbie, who came weekly to our house weekly and gave both Pat and I a massage every Saturday. I was getting my massage a week or so after the riding accident and told Debbie that my neck was still sour and she says she will see if she can correct it. She started to twist and turn my head when all of a sudden she gives it a violent turn and snap and all I can hear are things snapping either into or out of place. The result though is that the neck pain was gone. When I later tell a doctor friend of mine about how I got my neck was fixed he just looked at me. It seems that if Debbie hadn't done this maneuver just right I could have been paralyzed for the rest of my life. Good thing I didn't know that before the massage started.

The Embassy had a summer camp in Kashmir and every summer the Embassy staff headed north for some rest and relaxation at this tented camp in the mountains. The camp had all the comforts of home and Embassy staff could spend 1-2 weeks there enjoying the views of the Himalayas and a nearby glacier. Streams ran throughout the area and it was some of the best fishing in India, although I never managed to catch anything. Day trips were done on small mountain ponies, who as a whole were fairly slow animals unless the guide decided to crack them on their ass with a stick and then they barreled down the roads at lightning speeds and completely out of control. The only good thing was that the ponies were so small and low to the ground that all you had to do to slow them down was to extend and drag your feet on the ground. There were many small mountains in the area and one day I decided to climb one that didn't look too treacherous. Off I went and I managed to get to the top without any problems. The problem however was getting back down. I didn't realize that the hill had about a 45 degree slope and so I had to slide down the hill on my ass for fear that if I tried to walk down I would topple over and roll all the way to the bottom.

At night we had big campfires and sat out under the stars, which when you are in the wild and away from city lights, are intense. The other interesting thing we saw and watched were the large number of satellites that passed over this area of India, as often as every 5-10 minutes. The camp was in close proximity to China and so satellites from various countries were continually surveilling the area.

We had a number of cooks that came with the camp and so food was good and plentiful. One day I asked the cook if he could cook me a birthday cake as there were no types of ovens there, just a large wood fire. It was my wife's birthday and I thought it would be fun to give her a little surprise party. The cook managed to whip up what I estimate was about a ten pound chocolate cake that was the heaviest and densest cake I had ever seen. It did however taste pretty good considering what he had to work with. They brought out the cake after dinner and started to sing Happy Birthday and there my wife sat looking around trying to see whose birthday it was, completely forgetting it was her birthday at day. A moment later it finally sank in that the cake was for her and everyone got a good laugh out of that.

Another great trip was to the Pushkar Camel Fair in Pushkar, India. Pushkar is one of the oldest cities in India and tribes from all over the region converge on the city every November for the annual fair. Over 50,000 camels are brought to the city and traded or sold and camel races are one of the major attractions of the five day event. What made this event so much fun to go to was seeing all the colors on the people who attended it. Women wore bright outfits and all the men had brightly colored turbans that I believe denoted what part of India they had come from. One thing occurred at the Camel Fair that was noteworthy. We had traveled with a number of people from our Embassy by special train to the area and stayed somewhere in the immediate area. One of the persons that came with us was our neighbor's daughter who was visiting her mother at the time. When she got back to Delhi after the fair she noticed that she had a small bump on the tip of her nose that didn't seem to be going away and closer examination showed what appeared to be some sort of bite or infection. After a number of trips to the Embassy doctor it was determined that she had been bite by some sort of fly and that the fly had actually laid eggs inside her nose. The poor girl was then subjected to twice daily shots of some vaccine that had to be injected directly into the site of the infection on her nose. Ouch!! To subject this poor girl to even more unease and discomfort, it happened that there were only 3 documented cases of this type of infection. Doctors from around the world traveled to Delhi to take a better look at the girl's nose and further analyze the case. Happily the problem was rectified and the young lady was healed but not before the girl had numerous more injections into her nose and got back to normal.

By the time I had gotten to India I had become an avid runner and did daily runs around the embassy and though our neighborhood at home. One Saturday I felt fairly ambitious and decided to go for a run behind our house which was an area of sandy desert and woods. I started my run at about 1 p.m. and was soon gliding along through the wilderness and not really paying too much attention to where I was or where I was going. Finally I stopped to try to get my bearings and quickly realized I had no idea of where I was. I decided to continue running as I thought eventually I'd see some land mark that could help guide me home or I'd exit the woods and sand. Finally after about 3 hours of running I spotted the Qutah Minar, which is a soaring, 73 meter-high tower of victory, built in 1193 by Qutab-ud-din Aibak immediately after the defeat of Delhi's last Hindu kingdom. I knew that the tower was about 4-5 miles from our house and I also knew how to get back home from there. So with another 1-3 miles to go I reached the Qutah Minar and quickly set off for home knowing that I would eventually find my way back. About 3 1/2 hours had now passed since I departed our house and it was getting close to the dinner hour. Pat told the cook to get me up from my nap or wherever I was so I could get ready for dinner. The cook informed Pat that I had not come back from my run yet. To this Pat replied that was possible since I had left for my run over 4 hours ago. Upon checking the house she soon determined that the cook was correct and that I wasn't home. Finally after over five hours I came stumbling into the house and relayed my adventure to everyone concerned. That may have been the first unofficial marathon I ever ran.

India was famous for its shopping and one of the great things about living in India was that most of the time the sellers came to your house instead of you going to their place of business. Walla in Indian means a person who is engaged in a particular business, or a person who does something. Wallas came in all shapes and sizes and sold just about anything you could imagine. There was the silk walla, the stone walla, the picture walla, the clothes walla, etc. The stone wallas were particularly interesting, as they would come to your house with stone carvings that were several centuries old and try to sell them to you. When you examined the piece it was evident that the piece had recently been chiseled off some wall at a temple or building somewhere in India. One day I jokingly asked the dealer if he ever got any pieces from Khajuraho, which is a series of temples displaying erotic artwork and scenes from the Kama Sutra. He replied that he might be able to find something and would get back to me. About a week later he showed up with what looked like a freshly cut slab from Khajuraho. It is unfortunate that these wallas didn't realize how they were robbing from India's culture and art but they were in it for just the money. Khajuraho, which is a series of over 64 temples located in Madhya Pradesh, is a tribute to erotica and depicts numerous sexual positions between men and women among the thousands to figures carved into the sides of the temples. The various scenes of passionate love making, in acrobatic postures that sometimes border on the physically impossible although someone, at some time, had tried them. Similar temples can be found throughout India but none can rival the eroticism and beauty of Khajuraho.

Another thing one finds during his travels through India are naked holy men, who for a few rupees will administer a blessing upon you and mark your head with a red dot or Bindi. While we lived in Delhi it was fairly common to see naked holy men casually walking along the streets, sometimes accompanied by some of their followers. A common practice among women and occasionally men was the use of Henna to dye your hair. This gave it a bright red appearance that definitely stood out in a crowd. The Henna could also be used to create a sort of paste or heavy ink that was used during ceremonies to dye women's hands and feet. Once applied, the substance remained on your hands for several days before it finally worn off.

Indian food was unique and varied from region to region. When we first got to Delhi we thought we'd be eating all kinds of currie but quickly found out that curries were more from the Southern regions of India. When we asked the cook to prepare a curry for us he couldn't understand why we would want to eat something that was usually eaten by the lower class people in India. Delhi had a few curry restaurants but was better known for its tandoor food that was cooked in special ovens that reached several hundred degrees. This was usually served with dahl which are lentils cooked for extended periods of time on a stove. The good thing about eating these types of food in India was that any bacteria or bad stuff was definitely killed during the cooking process. One culinary experience was going to the most famous restaurant in Delhi, Moti Mahals. This was located in Old Delhi and upon arriving we had to walk through a sea of beggars and other people lying on the sidewalks outside of the restaurant. Once we braved the crowd outside we had what was a very traditional and delicious Indian meal. At the conclusion of the meal the owner came over and asked us if we would like to take a tour of the kitchen, as he knew we were from the American Embassy. Naturally we said, "Yes." A BIG mistake. The cooking areas of the kitchen weren't that bad and mainly consisted of a number of stoves with dahl and other items cooking along with tandoor ovens cooking the meats and Indian breads called Nan. What was a shock however was the dish washing area. There in the corner of the kitchen sat the dishwasher, barefooted, with a bucket of the dirtiest and greasiest water you had ever seen and washing the dishes and silverware that would eventually make its way back to the dining area. It is only a miracle that we didn't get sick eating here although most restaurants were fairly save to eat at provided you stayed away from any uncooked items or salads.

At home our cook had to disinfect all leafy vegetables and fruits in Clorox to ensure that things were clean for eating as the Indians used Black Gold, or human shit for farming and fertilizing vegetables, etc. Despite the dirt and grim of India we managed to stay fairly healthy for our three years there. Think Pat and I only got sick once or twice our entire tour. Most of the people who did get sick do so at home because their servants and cooks didn't follow good hygiene. One couple we knew decided that if they ate enough dirty or bacteria laden food they would eventually become immune to it and never get sick. This proved to be correct for them, however, whenever they had a dinner party, almost all the guests were out sick the next day. Eventually we found ways to regret to dinner invitations from this couple in order to avoid the Indian revenge.

We also had a tailor who made clothes for us while we lived in India. Most people brought cloth and materials with them to Delhi so that the tailor could fashion clothes for them. They were pretty talented and were able to copy just about any clothing item you might find in a fashion book. Since everyone else in India were wearing things made by their tailors no one looked out of place or out of fashion. The big shock came when you got back to civilization in Europe or the USA and then you looked like a refugee walking around in baggy and tattered clothing. This was really evident when we traveled back home on an R&R, Rest & Recreation, after we were in Delhi one year. The Embassy had a special deal with the Cunard Cruise Lines out of London whereby we could go home on the QE II from either England or France. The American Embassy had a stash of excess Rupees, which unfortunately for the Embassy could only be spent in India. Cunard agreed to accept the rupees as payment for American Staff members who wanted to sail back to the U.S. on the QE II for a five day crossing from either Southern England or France. A similar deal was struck with our Embassy in Cairo, Egypt. So off Pat and I went on leave via South Hampton, England, and we boarded the fashionable QE II for a five-day crossing back to the U.S. complete with First Class berthing. We took our finest Indian made clothes with us along with my Tuxedo for all those great formal nights on the ship. Other passengers and ourselves could immediately tell who were Embassy Officers from Egypt and India, as we all looked like refugees walking around on the ship in our tailor made Indian clothes. It was kind of like the movie, Titanic, where Leonardo DiCapro was in the third class section of the ship and his love was in first class complete with her jewels. One night I decided it was time to put the old Tuxedo on and didn't realize that I had lost so much weight after just one year of living in India. The tux looked like I had gotten it from my father or someone who was about two sizes bigger than what I currently was. The cruise was great however, the food was even better and in quantities you wouldn't believe. One morning Pat ordered bagels and cream cheese and the waiter returned with a dozen toasted bagels and a pound of cream cheese. Baked Alaska. Big enough for two, three, four, five, six, maybe even seven people. The sad part was that at night as we stood on the deck of this grand ship we watched as crewmembers threw garbage bag after garbage bag over the rear rails until there was a sea of floating black spots as far as the eye could see. I later wrote Cunard telling them how it distracted from our watching the sun set while we also watched their crew turn all those garbage bags into the ocean.

Pat and I also commented, after being in India for a year now, how that much food could probably feed lots of people on the streets of India. One of our dinner table companions was the Vice-President of Disney, who said that things had changed as far as ship travel was concerned. This was his wife's twentieth crossing and he said the service had gone continually downhill over the years. He said that in the old days if you were walking through a gangway and a crewmember was coming from the other direction, the crewmember would jump to the side and let you pass and maybe even throw in a salute. Now he said they would probably just knock you on your ass and keep going. Dinner service was good but sometimes a little shoddy. One morning I ordered Eggs Benedict with Hollandaise Sauce. The eggs came out fairly quick but I was done eating them when the Hollandaise Sauce finally showed up. It seems that the large cruise lines were used as a training grounds for the Merchant Marines and so the caliber of some of the waiters and help varied greatly.

There is nothing better however than arriving early morning in New York City on a large passenger ship and passing by the Statute of Liberty after being out of the country for a few years. It makes you think back to when our ancestors did the same on their migrations to the U.S.A. from their homelands. We arrived at the dock and cleared customs and my father was curbside with a stretch limo we had hired to drive us back to Pennsylvania. We had done a cost comparison between buying plane tickets for Pat and I to get to

Pennsylvania versus hiring a limo from Pennsylvania to drive us home and the limo was much cheaper at the time. It made me laugh to see all the people from the cruise looking at Pat and I getting into the stretch limo with its driver and wondering who the fuck those people were that were on their cruise and now was getting picked up right at the pier by a limo.

We headed back to Delhi after Home Leave for the remainder of our tour. We thought we'd have a year to go before bidding again on an assignment, probably Washington, as we had been overseas now for over 6 years. Turns out that later that year I put my bid in and then received a cable telling me about the great job I was doing in India and how they couldn't find anyone good enough to replace me at the moment, and so congrats, you are being extended another year in India. Keep up the good work. I shot a cable back to the folks in Washington telling them "thank you and I hope you remember your comments when the next promotions panel convenes."

As I mentioned earlier I was a Regional Security Officer and so besides four posts in India; New Delhi, Madras, Bombay and Calcutta, I also had security responsibility for Kathmandu, Nepal and Colombo and Kandy, Sri Lanka. Although Kandy was a really small post for the U.S. Government, it was the home of The Temple of the Tooth Relic, one of the most sacred places of worship in the Buddhist world. My assistant and I traveled to all these posts at least once a quarter or more frequently if something unexpected happened at a post. Travel was a major travel challenge back then. Today you can fly from Delhi to Colombo in a few hours. Back in the

80's it was a full day of travel and even flights to the interior of India took several hours to accomplish. Madras back then was, and continues to be, the Bollywood of India and makes hundreds of movies annually. In fact, next to the United States, India is and was the next biggest moviemaker in the world. Madras was also the single dry city in India and even foreigners couldn't get alcoholic drinks there. Nothing much happened in Madras work wise, as it was the smallest of my Indian posts. Bombay on the other hand was a fairly large post and the city itself was gigantic even back in the 80's. It took well over an hour to get from the airport to the Consulate, which was located in one of the busiest part of town. Other than some anti- American demonstrations nothing much happened there during my time in India. It was always a treat to travel to Bombay since I got to stay at the Taj Mahal Hotel, which was one of the best and oldest hotels in the city. It was also famous because of the well-known gate located just across the street from the hotel and used by the British when they finally left India after their rule. I also read in later years that there was a famous red light district just down the street from the hotel, which I somehow missed during all my trips to that city. The Taj would again become famous in 2008, when in the early hours of November 30th, Indian National Security Guard (NSG) commandos killed the remaining gunmen at this hotel, ending a three-day coordinated attack on the hotel and several sites around the city that ended with at least 195 people killed and almost 300 injured. The final push, after a gunfight through the night, was marked by heavy gunfire, loud explosions and a fire in a ground floor ballroom. Over 300 people would eventually be rescued from the hotel.

Calcutta was my fourth post in India and the second largest city in India and known for its poverty and masses of people who could be seen as one drove through the city. I stayed at one of the local hotels that became famous as Mohammed Ali supposedly stayed there one night and a photo of the boxing champ was proudly displayed in its lobby. Across the street was an old Chinese restaurant where I ate at on my first visit to Calcutta, didn't get sick from the food, and became my favorite and only restaurant for dinner when I visited. I figured if you didn't get sick at it, why go some place else, since this was India. Again, this post wasn't very exciting either work wise although one pretty interesting incident did take place there during my tour. It seems that one American Officer on the staff liked to skinny dip in the pool at the American housing compound. This would have been OK if it weren't for the fact that there were 7 other families living at the compound plus the Marine Detachment. Another important element was that the compound was surrounded by several high-rise apartment buildings occupied by Indian families and they had a perfect view of the swimming pool and the people who frequented it. This officer also decided that maybe some of the other diplomats in town who he entertained at his house might also like to partake in some good old nude swimming after they finished their dinner. On one such night he and his friends are all in the buff and having a good old time at the pool while having a few more drinks to boot. One of the Marine Security Guards decided to join the festive group, not knowing that everyone is completely naked.

The Marine comes running to the pool and proceeds to dive into the pool, finally realizes that everyone is naked in the pool and takes his mind off the act of diving. The result was that he does a header into the shallow end of the pool, thereby breaking his neck, but fortunately not killing himself. The next day I got a message to fly immediately to Calcutta to investigate this unfortunate incident and see how this Marine could have done what he did. After a very brief investigation it quickly becomes clear that the skinny dipping activities were a quite common event at the compound, however, most people for some reason weren't aware of it. Investigation closed. Can't remember what happened to the officer in question although I think he continued to serve his country in Calcutta, but refrained from future naked activities at the pool. I think this may have put a real dent into his social live as I heard the group he traveled around with were what we now call swingers.

NEPAL

Kathmandu was my post in Nepal and a quick 45 minute flight from New Delhi. On a clear day you could see Mount Everest as you flew between the mountain peaks. I always wondered how the pilots managed to maneuver the aircraft through these passes, as most days were very cloudy and not very clear. It was a rare day when you could actually see Mount Everest. It was a little scary when you saw how close the plane flew to the mountain peaks and you just hoped that the pilot wouldn't jerk the control unexpectedly or we would become part of the mountainside. It was also funny flying Royal Nepal Airlines as they, unlike Indian Airlines, served alcohol, as soon as the plane took off. This meant that when the plane took off all the Indian customers grabbed the stewardesses and began to drink steadily for the next 45 minutes. Kathmandu is a relatively small town and you can probably walk the whole town and see everything worth seeing in about 1 1/ 2 to 2 hours. Back then it was also much dirtier than India, if you can believe that and more people tended to get sick visiting Nepal than visiting India. It was also at an altitude of 4,600 feet, which makes running and walking a bit of an effort. The religion is mainly Buddhist as opposed to Hinduism in India. It is famous for Mount Everest and back in the 80's climbing Mount Everest was a bit more of a feat than it is today when scores upon scores of climbers wait in line for the honor of hitting the top peak and saying they did it. Back in the 80's you could walk through the streets and in various shop windows was the mountain climbing equipment used by famous expeditions who came to climb Everest and everything was for sale. Only a hand full of climbers reached the summit back then compared to hundreds who do it today. One weekend in 2012 saw over 200 climbers lined up and waiting to reach the summit. Despite the high numbers of people completing the trek, many others fail and several still die trying to accomplish the climb.

One other thing Nepal and the Himalayas are famous for is the "Yeti" or the "Abominable Snowman." The Yeti or Abominable Snowman is reported to be ape-like and taller than an average human and is said to inhabit the Himalayan region of Nepal and Tibet. From early times people in Nepal claimed to have sighted the Yeti and expeditions were formed to search for the Yeti and either prove or disprove the legion. Numerous stories and even a few movies have been made concerning this elusive creature. During one of my visits to Kathmandu I saw a notice at the Embassy that a German pilot had spotted what he thought was a Yeti and that an expedition, complete with T-shirts, was being formed to look for him.

Nepal also has the Living Goddess, Kumar Devi, who lives in a building along the streets at Kumari Bahal and appears in her window daily for onlookers to see and for locals to worship. A young girl is chosen to be the goddess and she remains the living goddess until she reaches puberty, when she is removed from the position and another goddess is selected. The goddess is carried through the streets of Kathmandu as her feet cannot touch the ground and she leads a life of seclusion. Many of the ex-goddesses eventually become prostitutes in order to get by. Religious ceremonies regularly take place in Kathmandu, many of which entail the killing of a cow or goat. Small temples line the back streets and larger Buddhist temples, including the famous monkey temple, are located on the outskirts of the city.

Another common factor in both Nepal and throughout India are the various ways in which the death is addressed. In Nepal it was fairly common to see a Buddhist priest setting up a funeral pyre along the river and preparing a body to be burned. The bones and remains are then dumped into the river. Many times if you look just down river you will see people bathing or washing their clothes in this same water. For the deceased it marks the moment when the transition begins to a new mode of existence within the round of rebirths. Many of the Buddhist and Hindu followers believe in being reborn as either another person or perhaps even an animal or something as simple as a bug. In India we also saw the dead placed on burial pyres, or as they are called, "The Ghats." The bodies are then either burned, with the remains falling into the river or left on the Ghat for the buzzards to come down and eat what remains of the body. Varanasi, India, has nearly 100 ghats, steps leading to the banks of River Ganges. The Ganges is a very sacred river and while bodies are being burned at one site, people are down river washing, or in some cases drinking the sacred river water.   Another common site around Kathmandu are the famous Gurkha soldiers who are posted in Nepal. Gurkhas are closely associated with the Khukuri, a forward-curving Nepalese knife and Gurkhas are well known for their fearless fighting in battle. They can be seen in town riding in mule drawn conveys as they move equipment and supplies through the city. In later years they would be found at many of our foreign service posts thought the world as part of the guard force because of their fearlessness and reputation as great fighters.

Another popular visitor's spot in Nepal was Tiger Tops. Visitors depart by small planes to a small grass runway about one hour from Kathmandu where they stay at this famous resort and have the opportunity to watch tigers in their natural habitat. On the first day of my visit we stayed in a stilted room high above the ground and ate our meals in a dining area on the lower level. We boarded elephants and rode through high elephant grass in search of tigers and rhinos that inhabit the jungles there. You don't realize just how high and how big an elephant is until you're sitting on top of him and moving through the brush. You also don't realize just how fast an elephant can move once they get rolling. The driver sat on the neck of the elephant and had a small steel type hook that he used to control the animal. When the elephant didn't do as the driver wanted, he would crack the elephant on the head producing the type of sound you'd get if you hit a coconut with a steel object. Needless to say this did get the elephants attention and he followed the rider's orders after that. At one point we saw a rhino with its baby and the driver and the elephant headed out in pursuit. We followed the rhinos for a while until the mother finally decided that enough was enough and she turned and charged the elephant. This sacred the hell out of Pat and I but merely produced a slight chuckle from our driver. On the next day of our safari we headed down river by canoe and to a different camp. This camp consisted of a tented area by the river and an open mess area for our meals. This area was where we were introduced to the tigers that ventured out into a nearby river to cool down during the day and just lay around for hours on end. We returned later in the day to the same location but the tigers had not returned. The people who ran the camp decided it was time to take action and they tied a goat to a stake in the immediate area of the river. A few minutes later the tigers returned to have a late day snack before retiring for the evening. Day three was more of the same and then our flight back to Kathmandu.

Our Embassy in Nepal was typical and had routine security problems but nothing major at the time. It was only in later years that the Maoist movement would take over the area and cause problems for the

Nepalese and result in increased security concerns at the numerous embassies in town.

SRI LANKA

The last post that I covered out of India was Colombo, Sri Lanka, which at the time took me about a full day to travel to. Colombo was a sleepy little town and situated along the ocean. It was a haven for European tourists who flocked there over the winter months. I still remember staying at an upscale hotel just up the street from our Embassy and seeing the topless German women at the swimming pool and along the beach. There were numerous signs advising tourist that topless swimming was illegal and punishable by a fine, however, the police officers patrolling the areas seemed to turn an eye away or maybe toward the topless women and no fines were ever given out to these foreigners. The waters along the coast were loaded with all kinds of tropical fish and one time when I went diving I sat in a coral garden and just watched all the fish you would see in a pet shop, swimming around me. Unfortunately I would return to Colombo several years later after I retired and was doing TDY assignments for DS and find that most of the sea life had been killed because of all the pollution along the coast.

The conflict between the Sri Lankan Government and the Tamil Tigers was in progress during this period and India was attempting to assist with controlling the rebels. The Liberation Tigers of Tamil Eelam, commonly known as the LTTE or the Tamil Tigers, was a separatist militant organization that was based in northern Sri Lanka. Founded in May 1976 by

Velupillai Prabhakaran, it waged a secessionist nationalist campaign to create an independent state in the North and East of Sri Lanka for Tamil people. This battle would continue for close to thirty years and finally got resolved in 2010. Fortunately while the conflict pursued, the Tigers didn't target the American Embassy and viewed us as kind of a neutral party to the events taking place.

When I returned to Colombo years after retirement as a rehired annuitant the city was a completely changed place. Roadblocks were all around the city and from the airport along the roads into the city and suicide bombings were a common occurrence in the capital. The President's House was just up the road from our new Embassy and police were stationed in force throughout the city. The country had expended close to $300 million fighting the enemy that left the country in disarray because almost all the country's budget was being used for the conflict. The Tamil Tigers were a determined group and recruited heavily from the local populace and were fairly successful in this venture. Recruits were trained for over a year in basic military tactics and were well aware from the start that some of them had been selected to be suicide bombers. Most attacks on local police, politicians and even the Sri Lankan President were usually successful and resulted in their targets either being killed or greatly maimed. One attack that took place right before one of my last visits to Colombo. A woman suicide bomber was used as women had became more and more popular to use in such attacks as local culture sometimes prevented local authorities from adequately screening people. The woman, wearing an explosive vest with ball bearings laced through it, approached the President

Nicholas Mariano

during a speaking stop. When she finally was challenged by one of the President's staff she detonated the device killing several people and injuring the President, to include her losing an eye. The President was not killed as luckily she was standing behind her armored car and the vehicle absorbed the major part of the blast. The vehicle did however look like a piece of Swiss cheese as the vest contained a large quantity of ball bearings that had almost a shotgun effect on everything in proximity to the bomber. The bomber's head was found a distance from the blast. Authorities can usually tell if it is a suicide bomber as the blast from the explosive vests almost always decapitates the bomber. One might ask themselves why anyone would train for over a year full knowing that eventually they would be killed carrying out such a bombing. Sometimes it is ideology or culture as we currently see in the Middle East today. Other times it is the promise of reward in heaven such as the Kamikaze pilots during WW II. In the case of the Tamil Tigers it was a combination of factors. The recruits selected to be suicide bombers were first elevated from basic Tamil Tigers to White Tigers, which gave them additional prestige among the Tiger Corps. They were also told that they would go to heaven for carrying out their attack, that they would be honored and always remembered by their fellow Tigers. Lastly, their parents would be taken care of for the rest of their lives. The last factor was especially important when you consider the poverty level of the average Sri Lankan at the time. Needless to say they had no problems recruiting Sri Lankans for their cause and for carrying out suicide attacks. Their organization was perhaps one of the most successful in the world. I should also mention that after the recruits had received their training and had a final going away celebration, they were placed back into society where they would then spent up to a year figuring out how to carry out their attack on a particular person that had been targeted by them.

The average person doesn't realize how complicated and well planned some terrorist attacks are. When I teach classes for the State Department's Antiterrorist Training Section, I tell my students to remember two things about terrorists. The first is, "Terrorist are Not Dumb!" Quite the contrary, most have college degrees and are well educated and from middle income families. Secondly, they have the advantage. They are in no rush to do their attack. When you look at the 9/11 attacks in New York and Washington, you see that these attacks required a great amount of training and planning. The same is true of the Nairobi Embassy bombing, where we saw that the attackers had been in country for perhaps a year or longer. They also know what kinds of technology the good guys are using as our friends at local news agencies are always ready to tell them about the latest technologies we are using to defeat terrorism and even sometimes tell them what the vulnerabilities of such systems are. Terrorist also look at other attacks throughout the world by their organization and other terrorist cells, to see what worked and what didn't. If it worked once, then maybe it'll work again. So in the case of Sri Lanka we were fortunate that the Tamil Tigers had only one enemy and that was the Sri Lankan Government.

Let's get back to India. As you read this you may start to think, when did this guy work? He's writing a lot more about visiting places, vacations, ship cruises and hitting dinners and parties. Yes, the Foreign Service does have all that but it also has its drawbacks and dangers. Pat and I spent 11 years living overseas, away from our friends and family, away from American culture and what was happening at the time. Some days we didn't have electricity or water, we got immunizations for the wide variety of diseases we might come across and ate foods that gave us the shits for days. Water had to be boiled in some cities, in India all fresh fruits and vegetables had to be soaked in Clorox. Mosquitos carried malaria and food contained parasites. Sometimes the cures for these diseases were worse than the disease itself. In Turkey during the winter months we had to run air purifiers at the office and at home because the Turks burned bituminous coal and when you woke up in the morning you had rings of soot around the nostrils of your nose. Plus, people did get killed serving our country and will continue to get killed doing so. We've seen this recently in a number of places around the world.

I should perhaps describe a little more about what a DS Agent does in the US and what he does as a Regional Security Officer overseas. Domestically we protect the Secretary of State, Foreign Dignitaries below Head of State, do passport and visa investigations, train foreign police on a variety of topics, train Foreign Service Officers going to high threat posts and an array of other things. Overseas, the Regional Security Officer (RSO) runs the security of our Embassies, now numbering well over 300 worldwide. He trains and supervises the local guard force, supervises the Marine Security Guards, and is responsible for the Physical, Procedural and Personnel

Security at overseas posts. Sometimes there are a number of RSOs at post and other times there is just one. So as you can see, we did work a lot in between the occasional party or vacation. There is no such thing as an 8am to 5pm job when you work for the U.S. Department of State Department. Overseas you are on duty 24 hours a day, 7 days a week and 365 days a year. You may not get paid for all those days and hours but you can be called to work them at a moments notice. It's a great career but it can take its toil on people who are a part of it. I pride myself that I am still married to the same women some 40 years later as one of the biggest drawbacks for working in the Foreign Service is a high rate of divorce. How many women do you know who would want to get dragged to some shit hole country and be a second class citizen? They cannot work in that country or travel unaccompanied, and must still be a happy camper. One advantage I had while working at State was that none of my overseas postings were truly terrible but there are many really bad places you can be assigned to. After I retired I managed to travel to some of them as a rehired annuitant and could only think to myself, "God I'm glad I was never assigned here when I worked at State full time" I could manage this place for 4-6 weeks but 2-3 years here would suck.

One of the biggest things that took place while I ran security in New Delhi, was the defection of a very high ranking individual from a country I won't name. It turned out that he walked into the Embassy one day and asked for asylum. We got these guys all the time and 99 times out of 100 it was some nut job or someone who had a legitimate gripe but wasn't someone that we would grant asylum to. This was that hundredth time when the guy turned out to be a prize catch. Shortly after he got into the Embassy we began to notice a marked increase in activity at one of the adjoining embassies and it appeared that a wide spread search was already underway for this person. The person was debriefed by several people at the embassy and it was determined that he had a real value to the U.S. Government and so he was whisked out of the country by some very ingenious means and ended up providing our government with a wealth of information including the identity of one U.S. Government employee who had been turned by this foreign government. It was the kind of story that books are written about but also an incident that doesn't happened everyday or even in the entire career of your average DS Agent. Without getting into the particulars of the case I can say that it eventually received a lot of news coverage when the person defected back to his home country and we realized that he might have actually been a double agent.

Back to some local customs. Weddings in India are something to behold. Before the wedding ceremony the poor groom is paraded through the streets sitting on top of a white horse and decked out in ceremonial garb complete with a crown on top of his head. A band usually leads the procession, followed by friends and family, as they march through the streets of his neighborhood. The band plays and neighbors cheer while the poor groom sits there wishing this was all over. The actual wedding reception was usually held at a local hotel or open field and entailed lots of food and drinks. I attended the wedding of my senior investigator's daughter and something really unusual, at least to us but not to the Indians, happened. About half a dozen transvestite/gypsies appeared at the wedding in their best outfits and approached the bride and groom's fathers to inform them that they required some money from each so they would not curse the newly wed couple. I thought it was kind of funny but my chief investigator considered this a very serious matter. He proceeded to negotiate with the outsiders and finally reached some type of agreement so that they were happy. No curses were placed upon the young married couple and they could now lead a happy and productive life. As long as we're talking about marriage and weddings I should mention another fairly common practice in India. Brides are expected to produce a dowry in order for the marriage agreement to be formalized. In India, dowry is the payment in cash or some kind of gifts being given to bridegroom's family along with the bride. Generally a dowry includes cash, jewels, electrical appliances, furniture, bedding, crockery, utensils and other household items that help the newlyweds set up her home. The problem arises when the bride and her family are unable to produce the dowry or the groom's family considers the dowry inadequate. In 2001 nearly 7,000 dowry deaths were registered in India over inadequate dowries, apart from other mental trauma cases. Bride burning, inducing supposed suicides, physical and mental torture by the husband or in-laws is sometimes found to be done if the bride fails to bring in a sufficient dowry. It was fairly common to read in the Indian newspaper about how some unfortunate bride or bride-to-be was cooking and just so happened to catch herself on fire and die. Laws have been passed to prohibit this practice but the custom still persists to this day. Just as the Caste system will always be a part of India, bride burning will also take place irregardless of what laws are passed in India.

The Soviet invasion of Afghanistan was taking place while we were assigned to Delhi and several Regional Officers had the opportunity to visit our Embassy in Kabul during this period. At one time Kabul was known as one of the party posts in the Foreign Service and competition was fierce to bid on assignments there. As the war continued there large numbers of Afghan refugees fled the country with only the bare essentials. They were not allowed to carry any large sums of money when existing, however, they could take personal belongings with them and so many brought Afghanistan carpets with them over the borders of India where they sold them for cash. A number of our people were able to get some really old carpets during their visits to these areas and our carpet collection still includes one or two such carpets. I had the opportunity to visit Afghanistan about two years ago on a ATA teaching assignment and was able to visit what I call the Russian Bone Yard, which is a several hundred acre area filled with all the discarded Russian military equipment that the Soviets decided to leave when they vacated Afghanistan rather than trying to move it back to Russia. The area goes on forever and is covered what every type of military vehicle that you can imagine. We laughed as we were going through it as we said this will probably have discarded American equipment here someday.

It is interesting to read that the Afghan people have never been defeated by a foreign army and even the Soviets with their brutal tactics were finally forced to leave the country or continue to have their soldiers killed in large numbers. The one thing I remember about Kabul was the T-shirt someone brought back for me from the Marine House at our Embassy. It had a picture of the Marine Corps bulldog complete with a DI's Hat and kicking the Russian Bear in the ass. If only I still had this shirt now but it has gone by the wayside like many other things during our twenty years of travel and moving with the Foreign Service.

The Marines are famous for designing T-shirts for their Detachments located around the world at most U.S. Embassies. Foreign Service personnel can accumulate 100s of these shirts during their career. One shirt designed by the Marines in Beijing many years ago said it was from the Red Ass Saloon at the Embassy. When the Chinese discovered that the Marines had named their saloon as such and that the Embassy had condoned the name, they were all PNG'd out of China and DS had to send a number of junior Special Agents into China to take their place and stand watch at our Embassy there.

Embassies are always getting famous people coming through for one reason or another. In The Hague we didn't get a famous person as much as a famous thing. I was assigned to meet and protect a man from the U.S. Postal Service who was carrying the famous "Moon Stamp", which was the original stamp taken to the moon by one of our astronauts and was now a "One of a Kind Stamp." The stamp was priceless since there was no other like it. The biggest celebrity to come to New Delhi was none other than Mohammed Ali. He was in India for some reason that I can't remember and for some reason President Carter decided to appoint him a Special Envoy and asked him to travel to Africa on some kind of mission for the U.S.A. One night Ali decided to come to the Marine House and spent several hours talking and joking with the employees at Happy Hour and also posing for scores of photos including a number of him punching someone, for make believe of course. It was a wild time at the Marine House and everyone had a ball getting to meet this famous personality. What makes this story a bit humorous though was what happened after he departed for Africa on his mission for the President. Ali came to the Embassy for a number of briefings and then I believe a U.S. military plane was dispatched to Delhi to transport him and his entourage to Africa to carry out his mission. After his group had departed, the Oberoi Hotel contacted the Embassy to advise us that the Ali group had departed and left several thousand dollars of unpaid bills at the hotel including, if I remember right, a $5,000 room service bill. The Embassy investigated the matter and the room charges and it appears that the group figured that since they were now special envoys for Uncle Sam, everything rung up at the hotel after that point was on Uncle's dime. I can't remember who finally paid all the bills but I'm pretty sure it might have been us.

I had mentioned the war in Afghanistan and should add here that the Iran hostage release took place while I was in Delhi and many of the released hostages were flown to Delhi where they were checked out before heading back home after their trying ordeal. Makes you think sometimes when you're overseas, as you never know what might happen at your post of assignment.

Speaking of the Soviets again, here's another little tidbit that happened when my parents decided to brave it and visit us in Delhi. Somewhere during their stay with us my father met the Press Attaché from the Soviet Embassy while he was walking our Afghan Hound, Boris. He would come home almost daily and tell us how he met his buddy from the Soviet Embassy while on his walk and then they would have either tea or vodka, depending on the time of day, at the Attaché's House that was just up the road from our house. As I mentioned before, dad had a knack for making friends during his visits to our postings and I wasn't sure if this was an accidental encounter or if the Soviets were trying to target me through my father.

Mom on the other hand was just happy to visit with us wherever we were posted and when she came to New Delhi I think she thought she had fallen off the end of the world. She couldn't see how anyone could possibly love being assigned there and prayed everyday that Pat and I would again be posted back to the civilized world. Whenever we rode in my car around Delhi she sat in the back seat and looked out the back window so that she wouldn't have to look at the beggars and lepers and other sights of India while we were driving. She managed to survive her one-month stay with us and the final straw that enforced her dislike of India happened as my parents were departing India. We had gotten my parents back to the airport and since I had security passes I was able to get them as far as the screening area before I headed back to the Embassy; sure that they would have no problems beyond that point. Wrong! It seems that somehow while mom was going through the security check she lost, misplaced, or had her U.S. Passport stolen from her purse. In any case, I received a frantic telephone call from my dad telling me that she couldn't get on the plane without her passport. Fortunately a friend in the Consular Section was able to call the authorities at the Airport and arrange for her to depart without a passport provided that my father vouched for her and confirmed that she was his wife. She finally made it back safe and sound to the U.S.A and after a score of paperwork and payment of $300 was able to get a new passport, although at this point I was sure her days of venturing outside the state of Pennsylvania would be extremely limited.

India had an antiquities law that stated what could and could not be exported out of the country. Obviously old statutes, paintings and certain artwork fell under this law although old automobiles also fell under this law at the time. A number of Embassy officers had bought old automobiles during their stays in India. There were a large number of old Ford Model- Ts and old British sports cars to be found at fairly inexpensive prices. One officer I knew bought an MGTD and had it completely restored inside and out. It broke his heart that he would have to leave it behind when his tour was over in India. Being industrious, he decided to have it completely disassembled and packed in crates along with his household goods so that he could take his beloved car back home with him. This was done and a few days after the car was completely disassembled and crated, the Indian Government decided that automobiles no longer would be included within this law. This tended to piss off the officer since he still had to find someone to reassemble the car once he got back home although at least he would have his beloved MGTD.

When it came time for employees to depart post we were informed that all items had to be inspected by Indian Customs before they could be packed up. This caused some people to sweat a little as they might have some questionable items being readied for shipment. This inspection could however be circumvented by paying around 500 rupees to the Customs Officials, who just turned a blind eye and signed off on your shipment without ever coming to your home. The same was true for getting Boris out of India. The Indians never looked at the dog's vaccination certificate when we came into the country but you needed a mountain of signatures and papers to get him out of the country. The Indians didn't care if you brought rabies into India but you better not take it out of India to some other country. Again, a quick payment of several hundred rupees and all the paperwork was completed without haste.

I had mentioned we had been extended in New Delhi for another year and finally after three years it was time to start packing things up and getting ready for another assignment, probably back to the U.S., as we had been overseas for over seven years at that time. At the time we were getting ready to leave officers from the various embassies were able to sell their household belongings to the general public. That rule changed just after we left Delhi. You could also sell your car to the Indian Government. If you brought a brand new vehicle into India when you arrived, the Indian Government would buy it from you for the exact amount of money that you paid for it. It made no difference how many years you had spent in India or how many miles were driven on the vehicle. If, however, it was a used car when you brought it in, the Indian Government would still buy it but at some outrageously low price. You could sell it to another diplomat but first you had to obtain the necessary paperwork from the Government, which took its good old time in getting it done.

Before our big house sale we were contacted by a local person who bought items from foreign diplomats. He told us he was interested in buying anything we had to offer for sale. I should mention that all foreign goods and vehicles imported into India were subject to a 100% Government tax at the time plus many foreign items were almost impossible to get on the local market. Anyway, the buyer shows up one night with his sidekick who had two very large suitcases completely filled with rupees. The buyer moved from room to room shouting out numbers for things he was interested in buying. Blender-$50 equivalent in rupees. A broken blender-$45 equivalent. But that doesn't work. Who cares, I'll take it. All the clothes you never wore any more as you had lost 30-40 lbs. while living in India. Video game-$250, B&W TV set-$300 and so on. As quick as I told the guy it was his, his sidekick would open the suitcase and count out the appropriate amount of rupees and pass them to me. The big sales item of the day was over a year's worth of old Playboy magazines. This was something you just couldn't buy in India because of customs, rules and the religious aspects of the country. So for 12 issues of Playboy-$325. I thought to myself, "Why didn't I get a subscription to Hustler too?" After traversing the house twice he packed up his goodies and I was left with enough rupees to fill my own suitcase. We still had a lot of stuff that we would have normally thrown out if we were moving around back in the U.S.A. but would sell those items at the big home sale. An ad was put into the local paper saying there was a big house sale at our address. We were advised by my locals to hire at least 3-4 guards to maintain law and order and so the sale began. At 8:00 a.m. The morning of the event there were about 100 plus people jammed against the gate of our house waiting for their chance to rummage the Mariano House for all those American goodies. The guards kept the gate chained and shut and admitted people one at a time while keeping the masses out on the street. Everything sold. Clothes that didn't fit. Empty liquor bottles that were a big item in India. It seems that Indians will buy an empty bottle of say Johnny Walker and then fill it up with colored water and proudly place it on ta shelf in the living room, to be admired by visitors who are impressed that he has such expensive liquor in India. The buyer would never however offer a drink of his high-end scotch since it is really just colored water. But empty bottles were big sellers. My cook and houseboy always took the empties that we threw out and sold them for a few extra rupees whenever they had the chance. Finally, after about 4-5 hours the house was empty of everything that would have been normally thrown out or given away and we were several thousand rupees richer. One friend of ours had one of the first VCRs to make its way to Delhi that I think he paid $1,000 for at the time. At the end of his tour he sold the VCR and a number of movies he had gotten a while in India for more money than I got for my automobile, which at the time was only 5 years old. So after 3 years of what turned out to be a decent tour in India I headed back to the U.S. for a tour in the Domestic Operations Branch.

We decided to go back home on the QE II again and made preparations to take Boris, our Afghan Hound, on the plane to France and then on board the ship for our 5 day cruise home. We really had doubts after sending Boris out of India as the ground crews weren't the most efficient in the world despite the fact that they were working for Pan Am. These fears turned out to be justified as when we arrived in Europe the dog and his cage didn't come out with the rest of our baggage. We were told that we had to go over to another building about 2 miles from the airport to pick up Boris as he was assigned to the air cargo terminal. To make a long and sad story short, we finally got a ride to this building only to find out that Boris had died on the plane from unknown causes. Upon examining him it was quickly evident that he hadn't been put into the correct cargo area of the plane and had died from the cold and lack of oxygen. This was also confirmed when I put in a claim against the airlines and almost immediately received monetary damages from Pan Am without any questions being asked.

Despite the tragedy we finally made it back to New York City and were again met by my father and a stretch limo that transported us to Pennsylvania for some well earned leave before we heading down to Washington, DC, for my new assignment.

BACK TO THE USA & DOMESTIC OPERATIONS

So after almost 7 years we got back to the US and the State Department in Washington, D.C. and Domestic Operations. Back then Domestic Operations did domestically what our overseas branch did at Embassies. We were responsible for the physical, procedural and personnel security of the U.S. Department of State in Washington, D.C. as well as all the annex buildings in the Washington area plus regional and field offices throughout the United States. Currently DS uses its own police group to do security in Washington but back in the 1980s we still used the General Services Administration Police Force. Even though Domestic Operations supervised the GSA Police on a day-to-day basis they still got their marching orders from GSA. We were also responsible for the physical security of Main State as well as our annexes and as years went by Diplomatic Security became a leader in the development of physical security standards that were adopted by the rest of the Federal Government. Usually, however, this came after something bad happened somewhere and then we scrambled to patch that deficiency so it wouldn't happen again. Case in point. After our Embassy in Beirut was hit by a car bomb being driven by an employee, we started to screen all vehicles entering Main State and our annexes and also decided some sort of physical barriers were needed around our buildings. Government agencies first thought that we should just close off all the streets around key buildings like the State Department and White House but the City of the District of Columbia would have nothing to do with that since they were all main streets used throughout the day to get around the city. Next idea was to put some kind of barrier around the building to stop a car from driving into the building. When we proposed this to the administration, their response was, "Don't be ridiculous, no one can drive into the State Department building!" Fortunately I had an Agent working for me in Domestic Operations who had been around for quite a while and he told me how a diplomat from one of the embassies in D.C. had gotten drunk one night and actually drove through the plate glass windows at the Diplomatic Entrance of Main State, coming to rest in the lobby where our guards were. When this story got conveyed to the Administrators at State the problem was quickly resolved and we ordered a hundred or so concrete Jersey barriers, similar to what you see on highways, from a company in Virginia and by that Monday the entire State Department was closed off with concrete. Within 2-3 days all the main government buildings in D.C. followed suit, to include the White House and Capitol Hill. I don't want to say that we got copied a lot but we did. Later we installed Delta hydraulic barriers at the vehicle entrances at State and low and behold, everyone else in D.C. followed suit.

Diplomatic Security has an extensive technical security and engineering group who have led the way in formulating security standards and equipment which eventually gets copied by all the other U.S. Government organizations both domestically and overseas. Some of our standards on bombs and setback distances required to negate the blast from a car bomb were so good that the Russians even adopted the standards for all their embassies overseas.

Getting back to Domestic Operations, besides the guards and physical security, we issued IDs for all State Department personnel, adjudicated security violations issued to State Department and other organizations overseas, investigated security breaches, monitored the alarm systems at Main State and our annexes and made security arrangements for VIP visits to the State Department. It was a small office at the time but we managed to do a lot of work with the people we had. Since my time at Domestic Ops the office has grown three fold and still is doing what it did when I was there and then some.

I started out as the Assistant Chief of DO and eventually became the Acting Chief when DS failed to find anyone they liked to fill the head position. My division became notorious for becoming a dumping ground for Agents that no one else wanted for one reason or another. I would go to weekly assignment panels in the Director's Office and a person's name would come up for an assignment. The head of that office would tell the Director, "I don't want that person because he or she is worthless or he can't do the job." The response from the Director was always the same. "That's OK we'll assign him/her to Nick's Office in DO." Gee thanks Mr. Director. I few times I got mad and told the group, "If an Agent isn't suitable to do any job that Diplomatic Security has, then shouldn't we just get rid of him or her?" Ya, sure, that's the correct thing to do, however, I think I better explain the tenure process to those of you that aren't familiar with it. It's kind of like being a judge on the Supreme Court. Once you're on board, you're good for life. It's almost the same with people who work for the Government, at least it was back in the 1970-1980's. Once you got tenured, usually after 4-6 years or working, you were good for life. You might not get promoted ever again if you did a bad job, but you sure as hell weren't going to get fired either. That's how the system worked.

The joke among bosses when it came to bad secretaries was that the only way to get rid of her was to Promote her out of the job position and therefore out of your office. If you promoted a secretary and she was in a GS-5 position and she was promoted to GS-7, then she had to bid on an assignment in her grade bracket. So we promoted the bad ones so we could hopefully get someone better in our office. Sounds nuts, but that's how it worked. I think now they may fire people but to do that you had to document each and everything he or she did wrong for at least a year or more, in order to get your case reviewed. Most bosses had neither the time nor the desire to do that, so we just lived with things while knowing that in two years or so we'd be moving on and that person would be someone else's problem.

I must say however, that despite getting dumped with all the rejects of DS, none of them were really bad. Most did a great job for me, with little guidance or pushing, and some I even managed to get a few promoted which really pissed the Director off to no end. He asked me one time after promotions, when three of my folks got promoted, what the fuck I was doing. I asked him what he meant and he asked how the hell can those people get promoted. I told him they did what I told them and their evaluations were neither good nor bad, so the problem must be in the promotion system and not in what I was writing.

Speaking of evaluations and writing them, I used to get extremely pissed when I was told by my seniors that I should write my own evaluation for my boss and he would tweak it a bit for submission under his name. As I got along in my career, I told folks, "If I can write 20 evaluations then sure as hell you can write the half a dozen or so that you have to do. Isn't that what supervisors do? Give me a break and have some consideration for me and do what the fuck you're getting paid to do. That didn't go over well most times but I did get my point across and I did manage to get promoted to the top levels of DS, so I guess I wasn't entirely wrong.

Domestic Operations was originally located in the old section of the State Department, the part of the building that used to be the War Department way back when. As such, it was lacking a little when it came to heat in the winter and AC in the summer. Many a winter day I sat at my desk with my overcoat on all day and in the summer, since I couldn't strip down to my shorts and a T-shirt, sweated my ass off while hot air flowed out of the vents even though we were told the AC had been switched on.

On day one of the employees opened the vault room in our office and yelling and screaming followed. It seems that a rat had found its way into our vault room and ran out when the door was again opened. Another employee was coming in through the main entrance to our office and so the rat continued his sprint out the door and up the hall with 2 Special Agents is hot pursuit. In the end he managed his escape and lived another day in the hallways of the U.S. Department of State. Rats were a common sighting at the State Department building according to our guards who manned the various entrances throughout the day and night. The guards at the Diplomatic Entrance, the entrance used by VIPs and Foreign Heads of State, was particularly noteworthy. The guards told me they would watch the rats at night walking across the railing on the second floor and you really didn't want to walk too close to the building when doing your rounds outside at night for fear of getting attacked by the hordes of rats there. Till this day you will see rattraps strategically placed around Main State and other government buildings in D.C. in an effort to reduce the rat population. I had previously mentioned that we put some Delta Barriers at all the vehicle entrances at Main State and although they performed as promised, that is, they could stop a five ton truck in it's tracks, they did have some initial problems. We had a few incidents where people were driving into Main State's underground parking garage and the devices activated, supposedly by themselves according to the guards, and usually taking out the vehicle of some VIP visitor or Undersecretary of State, as opposed to your regular employee. One day one of my Agents was in the process of reaming out one of the guards for damaging an Admiral's vehicle as the guards continued to plead with him and stress that it had happened on its own volition. As my agent continued his scolding, presto!, the barrier popped up all by itself and the guard yells, "See!"

It turned out that the barrier had a resistor, which over a period of days or weeks, accumulated a static charge and finally the barrier would pop up on it's own. Not sure how it always managed to do so when someone was driving over it though. Similar incidents were reported around town and in one instance at the CIA, an employee was driving too fast and in the wrong direction, causing a loop detector to trigger and almost total his car and kill him. While putting a device into the Pentagon, the construction folks weren't aware of a subbasement below the driveway and once the barrier was installed it broke through and fell a fairly long way and came to rest in the subbasement. Overseas we had similar incidents plus many of the local guards who didn't always pay attention to what was going on and popping barriers while people were coming or going occurred quite often. On one trip to Colombo, Sri Lanka, it just so happened that it was the Ambassador's limo that fell victim to the barrier, making the Ambassador, and especially his wife unhappy campers, since she didn't really want to ride around town in just some ordinary car.

Back to my staff in DO. As I mentioned they were all good guys and gals and just as in my first stateside assignment, people messed around in the office when work was slow. One Agent, Mike, who has since passed away, was the King of the Jokesters. The Agent who ran the ID Unit liked to wear a bright red blazer to work and every time Mike came into work and Bob had that jacket on, Mike would walk up to him and say" Oh waiter, can I have a table for two for lunch." This would usually piss Bob off but got a lot of laughs from the rest of us no matter how many times he did it. When Bob wore his red blazer we just came to expect that Mike would do his routine. Mike also hounded another agent, who tended to wear low priced suits to work. Mike would leave ads on his desks regarding big sales in NYC and advertised 2 suits, 2 shirts and 2 ties for $99.00. Speaking of clothes. Back in the 70's and 80's most Agents didn't wear your traditional black or dark colored suits with white shirts and pin striped ties. There was no real dress code and Agent's wore what they thought was the style of the day, whether that meant bellbottom pants, checks, plaids or whatever was in at the time. Some of the combinations were something to see and a number of Agents became famous for their loud clothes that at the time they thought were really cool and in. Unfortunately, even back then, there was a lot of laughing going around when these Agents showed up on your protective detail. I remember when I first started on the protective detail for the Secretary, I was banned for permanent midnights because the Agent-in-Charge thought my hair was way too long and my clothes all too wild. Weeks later, after a haircut and a visit to the local tailor shop that catered to our Agents, I graduated from midnights to day time assignments and eventually even riding with the Secretary in his Limo.

Besides the Beirut bombing overseas, perhaps the biggest security incident to happen at State Department while I headed DO took place one Friday when I just so happened to be on leave. We had received a Memo from a woman working at State Department telling us that she was having problems with her son and that she wanted his State Department dependent ID revoked. It took about 2-3 days for the memo to reach us as we had moved our offices out of Main State and into a nearby Annex. One I should add that had heat in the winter and AC in the summer and thankfully fewer rats. We received her memo through the interoffice mail system, which wasn't the fastest in the world. We then sent it to the GSA police at Main State, which took another day. A notice was then put out to all the entrances to intercept this boy when he tried to come in again. Guards were given his photo, however, several thousand people pass through those portals daily and the chances of spotting him during rush hour was highly unlikely. The boy entered the Department via the employee's entrance carrying a bag that was not screened because he had a valid State Department ID. He headed to the floor where his mother was located, went into the men's room, assembled a rifle, and then casually walked down to his mother's office and shot her dead. All hell broke loose as to how this could have happened. As a side note. Our office had been trying for almost a year to persuade the powers to be that we needed to switch from having the guards eyeball IDs to installing an electronic ID card system with turnstiles at all the entrances. This was repeatedly turned down because it would cost Too Much!

The day after the unfortunate incident we again explained to the bosses that this could have been prevented if we had an electronic system installed at the time. We could have merely switched off the boy's ID card and when he tried to enter the building an alarm would have sounded alerting the guard, who could have stopped him at the entrance. This time we were told to get the access system installed ASAP. It's unfortunate that it took a death to get things done but in my career with the U.S. Government a lot of security things don't get fixed until after the shit has already hit the fan. This doesn't apply only to State Department but to the government system as a whole. It's just how we do things in out Government. People don't want to spend money on things that might happen but sure as hell they'll spend that same money after an incident does happen.

Eventually it was decided around Washington, D.C., that Jersey barriers weren't the most pleasing things to the eye and everyone embarked on ways to beautify their buildings while at the same time making sure a terrorist couldn't drive into their facility. Our office got together with GSA and we designed a series of barriers around the building that didn't look like barriers but were capable of stopping a car or truck loaded with explosives. While I can't get into the particulars of how the planters and benches, etc., were constructed at Main State I can assure you that they will stop any vehicles that might be used to attack the building.

After 9-11 we had to rethink how you protect a building but the idea of terrorists using airplanes to attack a facility goes back a lot further than the World Trade Center attack. We always envisioned that this was a viable form of attack but what we didn't envision was that terrorists would use passenger airlines to carry out such an attack. We were thinking more along the lines of a smaller privately owned type plane. These thoughts were enforced when a teenager flew a small plane into Russian air space and landed it in Red Square. The thing you have to remember when it comes to terrorism is that the terrorists usually have the upper hand. I stress this when I am teaching ATA counter-terrorism courses overseas. The terrorist know what has worked and what hasn't worked during previous attacks. They know some of the defenses that we employee at government facilities since the news media is always there to tell them about the latest and greatest counter measures we are employing on the evening news. The Internet contains a vast array of information that terrorists can use, including Google Earth, which will allow you to view your target and all the surroundings and roads so you can plan out your attack without even visiting the site initially. Plus terrorists are not in a hurry. They can plan something for next week or next year. In a number of attacks that took place at our facilities overseas we know that the terrorists were in country over a year before they carried out their attacks. The Internet can also provide you with all the instructions you need to build a bomb, whether you're a professional bomb maker or some high school kid planning to blow up your high school and classmates. A number of publications that came out in the 60's with detailed instructions on bomb making and other nasty things are still out there on the web. During one of the classes I was teaching on bombs recently I searched the Internet for the "Anarchist Cookbook and the Weatherman's

Cookbook" and not only could I download both publications as a PDF file, I could even buy a hardback copy of them from a store in England. That's why I am always amazed when someone asks me how a high school student could ever learn how to build a bomb. I think that government officials should stop worrying about how to stop porn on the Internet and instead concentrate on how to get information about terrorism and bomb making off the Internet. The other thing people don't focus on is that besides foreign terrorists we still have your garden variety domestic terrorists as seen when Timothy McVeigh attacked the Federal Building in Oklahoma City and killed 168 people, including a number of children at the day care center in the building and injured over 600. Windows over a mile away were blown out or broken. It appears that the entire attack was carried out by McVeigh alone and without any outside help. "The Lone Wolf." The most difficult type of terrorist to detect and stop. That is besides all the other organized domestic groups that we still have to worry about, ones we know that don't like us and are capable of carrying out attacks if and when they decide to so. In addition, throw in the nuts out there and you'll see just how hard it is for security officials to stop every possible type of attack that there is or that someone may dream up.

Look at the sarin gas attack that took place a number of years ago on the Tokyo subway system. This attack was carried out by a religious group in Japan and the Sarin gas was home brewed at their compound. Rumors from the past say the U.S. Army once released inert gases on U.S. subways to see how an attack might affect people on the subway. Then there are the attacks using devices and methods we haven't even thought about but perhaps the terrorists have. While I was heading DO there was an incident at the Washington monument where a truck managed to get up close and personal to the monument and the driver told authorities that his truck was laden with explosives. A quick calculation by my folks based on the size of the truck and potential types of explosives, including ammonium nitrate or fertilizer like McVeigh used in Oklahoma City and that is readily available to farmers and other users, revealed that a potential blast of that magnitude would blow out windows in the State Department and other government buildings several blocks from the monument. So you can see that some things are very hard to protect.

As I previously mentioned, DS and the State Departments folks have been on the forefront when it comes to developing counter terrorist methods and equipment that has become the gold standard for the entire U.S. Government and a number of foreign governments.

Following five years at Domestic Operations in Washington it was time for me to head out one more, and presumably one last time, overseas. When it came time to bid I put only two bids in even though we were required to put in 5-6. I told my boss that this was perhaps my last overseas tour and that I wanted to go someplace I wanted to go versus where DS thought I should go. So I bid on Geneva and Rome. I was told that Geneva was out as it had been promised to someone already because he had served at such a terrible post and that was his reward. I told my boss that it should then be an easy matter on where I go since I had served five years in DO putting out fires and should also be rewarded. Thus Rome was my chose. While not getting into how I finally got Rome I would only add that the Director never spoke to me again while I was still in D.C. because of the pressure I put on him in getting this assignment. Everything was above the board but the powers to be don't like having to bend to DS Agents, who demand things. So Rome it was.

ROME, THE VATICAN & MALTA

After working for DS for over 14 years I was assigned to the American Embassy in Rome as the Head of Security for Italy, The Vatican and the Island of Malta. My office covered Rome, Milan, Naples, Florence, Genoa, Trieste and Palermo in Sicily. We also covered the Vatican, which had it's own Ambassador and one of my Assistant RSOs assigned permanently to it. Valletta on the island of Malta also had its own Ambassador and was visited by our office on a regular basis. This was my first overseas assignment after spending about five years back at the Department and during that time things had changed quite a bit terrorist wise. Increasingly more terrorist groups were turning up, particularly throughout Europe and numerous attacks and incidents began to increase throughout the world. In 1981 US Brigadier General James Dozier was kidnapped from his apartment in Italy by men posing as plumbers. The kidnappers were members of the Red Brigades, an extreme left-wing terrorist organization that sought to undermine the Italian state and pave the way for a Marxist regime. Dozier headed NATO's Southern European Command and was the first American General to ever be abducted by terrorists. Dozier was held for 42 days and was finally rescued by an Italian Special Operations Team, The NOCS, and all his abductors were captured. I'll write later about the NOCS as our office worked a lot with them and we spent many a day at their beach training sites doing joint training and just having a good time eating some good Italian food and drinking wine.

The Red Brigade was also responsible for the kidnapping and assassination of Italian politician Aldo Moro in the 1970s. The Abu Nidal organization, a splinter group of the PLO, was becoming active in Europe and was responsible for numerous attacks there . The group was responsible for the Rome and Vienna Airport attacks in December 1985 and for attacks against the United States, the UK, France, Israel and numerous Arab countries. In 1984 the Red Brigade struck again in Rome when they attacked and killed Leamon Hunt, a U.S. Diplomat and the first Director General of the Multinational Force and Observers (MFO) in the Sinai. On February 15,1984 as Hunt arrived at his gated home in Rome he was attacked and although his vehicle was armored, one of the attackers was able to penetrate the car's protection by firing into the upper edge of the rear window. A bullet struck Hunt and he later died at an Italian hospital from a bullet wound to the head. This attack occurred before I arrived in Rome and when I later studied this attack I found out that when Hunt was attacked, his driver failed to try to evade the attack by reversing out of the driveway and trying to escape. Instead he ducked down on the front floor of the vehicle, thus escaping injury himself, while the gunmen continued to fire on the car. There was much debate about this attack but one positive thing did come out of it. Drivers for all American embassies and U.S. Government VIPs were then required to take defensive driving courses as part of the terms for their employment so that they were trained in evasive measures to take in the event they were attacked. This training is now given to all our Special Agents and embassy personnel going to high threat postings overseas. Having gone through this training a number of times I cannot speak too highly of its benefits both while living overseas but also when coming back to the U.S. and facing the crazy driving there that we sometimes have here. One of my former bosses was posted in Egypt and is alive today only because he and his assistant had taken this training and were able to evade a terrorist attack on their vehicle one day while on their way to work. They received minor injuries from the attack but are still alive to tell their story.

The American Embassy in Rome sits on an upscale downtown street, the Via Veneto, and has seen its share of history. The Embassy was once the home of Queen Margherita, the first sovereign of Italy. After her death in 1926, the Palazzo Margherita was partitioned into offices for the National Fascist Confederation of Farmers and later purchased by the U.S. government in 1946. Since then, the 300-year-old building has been carefully preserved and upgraded to meet modern security requirements. During the war it was occupied by the Fascists and Mussolini for a time until the allies liberated Italy and Rome. Mussolini installed marble tablets in the hallway of the second floor that were later covered over by hinged covers. It was also used by the allies as their headquarters during the war and remains our embassy today and an historic building on the Italian Registry.

Before my arrival there were only ornate bollards and heavy chains separating the street and side walk from the building. Following car bomb attacks in various parts of the world, the embassy requested that the Italian Government allow the installation of a strong metal fence around the chancery. The Italians denied this request because the building was a historic structure and therefore had to maintain its integrity as such. According to stories I've heard, the U.S. decided that it was more important to protect the embassy and its occupants than to protect the historic significance of the building. So one night according to stories, workers arrived with fencing in hand and presto, there was now a protective fence erected in front of the Chancery without the Italians approving anything. Eventually the Italians noticed that a fence had popped up over night or maybe several nights and requested that it be immediately taken down since "This was an Historic Building!" Well, that never happened and the fence remains in place till this day.

Back to Mussolini for a moment. Although many may look adversely at him and his actions during the war, he was responsible for some of the grander that is Rome today. He erected many of the ornate bridges, scenic parks and monuments throughout the city in an effort for Rome to become the seat of rebirth for the Italian empire. He was also responsible for building the Olympic Stadium on the outskirts of Rome, which opened in 1932, with seating for 20,000 and ringed by 60 colossal statutes of nude Roman athletes. During my stay in Rome I was lucky enough to run the Marathon of Rome which winds for 26.2 miles through the streets of Rome and The Vatican and goes past just about every famous site to be seen in Rome; the Spanish Steps, Villa Borghese Park, Trevi Fountain, the Vatican and several other famous tourist stops before finally finishing at Mussolini's stadium to the cheers of thousands of spectators. Many of the runners carried cameras with them and stopped throughout the race to take photos of all the famous sites. One interesting fact about the marathon that I won't forget. Close to 22 miles of the race are run over the cobble stone streets of Rome and the day after the race my feet had been punished to the max. I wore a suit and sneakers to work for the next 2 weeks before I was able to walk again in dress shoes.

As long as I'm talking about running in Rome I might as well continue on this topic a little more. Rome is heaven for runners and while I lived in Rome I ran almost every day. I ran from our house on the outskirts of town to Rome almost daily as it was much faster and less frustrating than trying to drive to work through the Roman traffic. I was able to face the workday with a more positive attitude after doing my 5-6 miles. There were races almost every weekend somewhere in town, which varied from 3 miles up to half-marathons. I managed to collect quite a stack of certificates and medals while stationed in Rome and came home the skinniest I had been since I was in high school. It also made me feel less guilty about eating pasta almost everyday, sometimes twice a day. Don't runners need all those carbs anyway? As I said, the Rome Marathon was a highlight of my running and since the race started about 3 p.m. and ended in the evening hours it was a great experience. I ran the race with a friend from the embassy although half way through the race I left him in the dust and ended up finishing the race in just over three and a half hours but with sore feet that wouldn't stop hurting for several days. The next week we both decided that since we were in such great shape, why not try an ultra marathon in a few weeks time?

We continued to train and decided to do the "100 Kilometer del Passatore" (66.6 miles). The race starts in Florence along the old Appian Way that was built in 312 BC and winds through the countryside for over 560 kilometers. The first 50 kilometers are all up hill and the last 50, all down hill. The race ends in Florenza, a city famous for its wines famous for its wines. What makes the race unique is that you have 24 hours to finish it and it winds through old villages along the route. Each village sets up tables along the way and provides mini-meals to the runners ranging from pasta and wine to meats, sandwiches and just about every Italian food you can imagine. It may sound strange but the food really tasted good after running for several hours. I never thought a good plate of spaghetti and a glass of vino would be something I'd want to eat while running an ultra-marathon but it gave us the energy to keep going. We even stopped along the way to catch some sleep at a small inn and rehydrate before starting out again the next morning. I still have the gigantic certificate and medal from this race hanging in my office today.

There was almost a race every weekend and so I never ran out of things to do while in Italy. One race was kind of funny during the winter. I had a water station coming up as I ran the race and reached over to grab a cup of water or so I thought. I almost burned my mouth off as they were serving hot tea at the station versus your normal water since it was wintertime. Biking was also really big in Italy and throughout Europe and one of my local investigators was friends with the mechanic of the Italian National Bike Team. He convinced the mechanic to build me a custom bike before I left Rome that I used for several years doing triathlons when I got back to the U.S.

I had five Assistant Regional Security Officers working for me in Rome plus RSOs in Milan and The Vatican, who came under my supervision. It was one of the larger Security Offices in the world at the time. One ARSO, Dick, had a photo of Ronald Reagan as Rambo hanging behind his desk along with a plastic Viking Helmet and battle axe. He also had a safe drawer filled with knives and Ninja throwing stars.

Another ARSO, Tom, passed his time by copying different photos from newspapers or books and then gluing either my face or that of the Ambassador on the photo and then either hanging the photos throughout the embassy or passing them out to employees. I really didn't mind my photo being passed out but I told him that both our asses would be grass if the Ambassador ever saw one of his works of art.

Then there was Leo who was assigned to The Vatican Embassy but longed to be over at the Rome Embassy, only a few miles away, instead of where he was. I visited Leo at The Vatican shortly after I arrived and was amazed at the size of his office as the embassy had been palace at one time. The room was huge and Leo's desk was about 10' wide and there was a gigantic crystal chandler hanging directly over it. I told him that I felt like I should kneel and kiss his ring when I first came in the room. Leo also stood out around the Vatican as he had an old Cadillac convertible that he drove around town in. We eventually closed the security office at The Vatican and I moved Leo over to the Rome Security Officer where he was a happy camper for the rest of his tour in Italy. He was also one of the best investigators in the office and was involved in two major cases, which I'll talk about later.

Then there was Dennis, who primarily provided protection to the Ambassador as it seemed that our Ambassador was confident that he was a prime target of Muammar Gaddafi following the U.S. bombings in Tripoli. Gaddafi said he was going to get our Ambassador and our Ambassador took this threat quite seriously. Dennis liked to wear a wool hat with earflaps during the cold winters and earned him the name "Elmore Fudd", fondly bestowed upon him by his buddy Tom.

Then there was Judy, our secretary, who was a party animal and had a large rubber arm and hand on her desk that was battery operated and waved to everyone as they entered our office. When my boss from Washington came to Rome for his yearly inspection he told me "Nick, you have a great office, however, some of your people have to get a little more serious." I passed this on to the staff after he left and was hit by a unified reply of "Fuck Him!"

When Pat and I first arrived in Rome we were assigned to a very large apartment just down the street from the Ambassador's Residence. The owner informed us during our initial visit that the apartment had previously been occupied by Rod Steiger and Claire Bloom, when Rome was the place for Hollywood movie stars to frequent. The place was huge, on the top floor of the building, and had a large patio complete with a brick bar-b-q just off the living room. The problem, however, was that most of the walls were painted bright purple and the rooms had a loud multicolored flowered pattern carpet throughout. There were two large baths, one black marble with all gold fixtures and the other blue marble with gold fixtures. The apartment was kind of cool but we told the landlord that something had to be done with the paint job and that the carpets had to go. The landlord replied that he couldn't do that since "if it was good enough for Rod Steiger and Claire Bloom it should be good enough for you and your wife". So the house hunt continued. Fortunately one of my local investigators knew an Italian politician who was retiring and moving to his farm on the outskirts of Rome and wanted to rent his elegant apartment on the outskirts of Rome. We went up to see the place and it was magnificent. Hardwood floors, silk wall coverings, and three bedrooms with balconies off all of them. The apartment was also filled with antique furniture that the owner said we could keep if we wanted any of it left in the apartment. So we ended up moving in. The owner and his son, a consignerie for the Italian Government, were great people and had us come to the father's farm almost every weekend that we wanted. He had a number of cows and farm animals and made homemade mozzarella di Bufala cheese that he brought to us weekly by the caseload. We finally had to ask him to stop as we accumulated so much we didn't know where to

153

put it or how to eat it fast enough. One Thanksgiving the father brought us a gigantic turkey that we had to saw in half and cook at two different houses as it was too big for your European style oven. We managed to feed the whole security office and the Marine Security Guard Detachment with this bird and still had some leftovers. A funny part of this dinner involved some home wine that my local investigator's mother made for us. As we drank it we noticed that it was staining everyone's teeth a reddish blue color. I began to fear that the stain might be permanent but thankfully the next day everyone's teeth were back to normal.   The first day we lived in the apartment I drove into work confident that I had memorized the route and would not get lost. Mission accomplished as I drove into the Embassy that morning. I can't say the same about coming home that night. Remember this was before GPS and cell phones. I headed home after work and it was starting to get dark but I was sure I had the route down. Eventually I ended up on a mountaintop somewhere on the outskirts of Rome with the entire city lit below me. I had no idea where I was or how the hell I could have gotten so screwed up route wise. I began to backtrack, made some corrections at a few intersections and eventually got back to the apartment that night and told Pat about the adventure I had. Thankfully, that was the first and last time I got so lost navigating to and from home.

We had two cars while we were in Rome, a brand new Alfa Romero and an old and rusted out Lancia coup that I had inherited from the previous security officer for the merger sum of $200. The Lancia was great for its age, the body was a little dull but had no major dents and it was great for dodging Italian drivers as who cared if it got hit. The only real problem the car had was that the drivers seat occasionally released by itself while I was driving and the back of the seat suddenly reclined into the back seat. This wasn't a major problem normally although it was sometimes difficult to see where you were driving as you were lying flat across the seat. It did result in some cursing, laughs from Pat and I and some quick action getting upright again whenever it happened. When we were ready to leave Rome a few years later I offered the car to my American and Italian staff for free but no one took my offer. I told my local investigator to junk it and found out that it would cost me $500 to turn the license plates in and scrap it. Given that I only paid $200 for it, I didn't intend to spend that much getting rid of it. I told my local investigator to take the plates off, as the car was never really registered to me, and then take the Lancia outside of Rome and park it in an alley with the key left in the ignition. This was done and till this day we will never know what happened to this great old car. Is it still sitting in some alley waiting for an owner to claim it or is it still roaming the roads of Italy somewhere?

As I mentioned at the start Leamon Hunt and U.S. Army General James Dozier had been targets of terrorists before my arriving in Rome as terrorism was becoming more and more prevalent throughout the world. We had continuous threat alerts and there were many a day when myself and the other agents sat at our desks working, with our handguns sitting on the desk and a shotgun and Uzi submachine gun sitting on the couch in my office. The police were constantly on alert because of general crime along with the increased terrorist threat. There was one incident where two police officers escorting an armored car were shot and killed and after this incident the police began to take extra precautions to ensure that it didn't happen again.

One day while sitting in my office we heard sirens and then gun shots from in front of the embassy right on the Via Veneto. We ran out to the front gate and asked what was happening and both the guards and police said that they must be making a movie on the Via Veneto as there was a police car chasing another car up the Via Veneto and one of the police officers was hanging out the window shooting at the other car. About two minutes later we saw about a dozen police cars at the top of the Via Veneto with guns drawn and looking like they were about to arrest someone. Turns out that an innocent civilian had gotten between a police follow car and an armored car carrying a large sum of money and when the police motioned and attempted to get this car out of the way the driver panicked. This only reinforced the thought that another robbery was about to take place. One of the police officers took out his gun and started waving it at the suspect car, further causing its driver to panic even more and try to flee. This further confirmed to the police that this was the real thing. After numerous attempts to stop the car failed, the police officers opened fire on the fleeing car causing the driver to speed up even more. Finally after a radio alert went out, the car was stopped at the top end of the Via Veneto and after several tense moments of conversation the matter was resolved and the person was allowed to go on his way.

Then there was the time that the Ambassador's vehicle was coming in via the front gate to the Embassy, and as guards were checking the vehicle for bombs, they noticed a mass of wires and a black box on top of the air cleaner as they lifted the hood to inspect the engine area. This prompted them to call the security office and myself and two other agents responded to the front gate for a look. Sure enough there were lots of wires and a black box sitting on top of the air cleaner and no one was sure what it was. As we discussed the situation and whether to call the bomb squad, along comes the embassy mechanic through the front parking lot, he walks up to the Ambassador's limo and before we could stop him, pops the car hood fully open and retrieves a metering device that he had forgot and left on the engine while servicing the vehicle. This was a great relief to everyone even though I think a few of us may have shit our pants thinking we were about to be blown sky high.

In my early days with Diplomatic Security, then the Office of Security, I was picked to go through the Navy's Improvised Explosive Device School with Seal Team Six at Indian Head, Maryland. It was a fun filled course where we learned all about explosives and devices and tried to take several devices apart without getting blown up. The practice devices were wired just like the real thing however, the actual explosive was located outside in a bunker. If you made a mistake while working on the device, there was a BIG boom and lots of dirt hitting the roof of the building you were in. Think my team was about 60% successful in dismantling our devices, however, it was the other 40% that would have killed you. After I graduated from this school I promptly assembled a bomb kit so that I was ready to tackle any explosive device that came my way and off I went to my first overseas assignment in Turkey.

In the early 70's and 80's there were no EOD squads at most police departments overseas. In some countries you may have a U.S. military base nearby with well trained EOD personnel but I remember many a time taking a suspect package or letter, X-raying it and then if it looked fishy, taking it to some remote spot and getting out my homemade bomb kit and taking that baby apart just like I'd been trained. Now that I am older, and obviously much smarter, I think back to these days and ask myself, "What were you doing?" But I was young and adventurous and a bomb guy having finished my training and never thought that this was NOT the thing to do. In later years at the State Department in Washington, DC, we screened the mail for the Secretary of State and did the same stupid shit. Now when I travel overseas doing work for the State Department's Antiterrorism Assistance Program and teach my module on bombs, I tell all my classes Two Things. If you're NOT an EOD expert and you can see something that looks like a bomb, You are TOO CLOSE! Get the hell out of there and call the guys who do bombs for a living. Also, the only way to be safe from a bomb is to put as much DISTANCE between you and it.

While I was stationed in Rome our office formed a great relationship with both the Carabinieri, who are the Italian military police and are responsible for protecting both the military and civilian populations and the NOCS, who were the special ops guys with the Italian State Police. The Carabinieri were the guys that all the tourists see around Rome with their traditional and distinct uniforms and hats. The NOCS are the guys you only saw during high threat events; all young, very handsome and super well trained. When they not involved in some real work, they just train and train. We got to known them quite well and went with them about every week to one of their training sites outside of Rome and along the sea. Before we left we stocked up on some vino and good Italian cold cuts and breads so that after a full day of training we could sit by the water and have some good food and wine at the end of a busy day. Getting to the training site was perhaps the most dangerous part of the day, not because we were carrying cases of ammo and some explosives, but because they drove to the site like they were going to a fire. Lights and sirens on, passing cars coming and going and getting a good laugh to boot since they could tell by the expressions on our faces that they were scaring the shit out of us. Once we got there though it was a great day of training, shooting our weapons, their weapons and occasionally blowing up something at the site that looked like it should be blown up. The day ended with a nice meal on the beach and then another, a not so quite scary, ride back to Rome.

We did have a few terrorist incidents during my stay in Rome but fortunately none where people were killed. There was a car bomb just across the street from our compound, that fortunately didn't cause much damage or kill anyone as the bomber wasn't very good and 90% of the blast from the explosion went straight up in the air so that even the car parked right behind it had only very minor damage to it. Think all that really happened were some windows at an adjacent hotel got broken and some black soot was left on the outside of the building. It did get everyone's attention and as a result security was heightened for a while.

About a week later a fairly new and expensive Mercedes was seen parked across the street from the rear gate of our embassy in a "No Parking Zone" that had been set up by the police as a result of the bombing the week before. An alert guard at the embassy notified me at the security office and we called the Italian EOD guys to come out and check it. The bomb people arrived, checked the car over and decided they had to get into the car and especially the trunk to make sure this wasn't another bomb. So they placed some small explosive charges on the Mercedes to breach the door and trunk. As they were doing this the owner was returning to his illegally parked car (hey this is Italy, no one pays attention to signs here) and when he saw the police and bomb folks all gathered by his car, he began to run toward us yelling for us to stop whatever we were doing. Too Late! Boom, pop, the door and trunk were blown by the charges and now wide open, with a fairly good bit of damage to the car. When the owner finally arrived yelling at everyone about his car, the Police, who had quickly checked the car over, told him that he shouldn't have parked in a "No Parking Zone" and merely turned and departed the area, while the owner was on the verge of tears.

Then there was the rocket attack at the Embassy while the Economic Summit was taking place in Venice, Italy. Seems that some bad guy scouted out the embassy with the intension of firing homemade rockets at the front entrance of the embassy around the time all the employees were coming to work in the morning. We believe he watched the embassy from a hotel across the street from the embassy the week prior to the Summit taking place in Venice and saw numerous people coming and going through the front gate between 8:00 am and 9:00 am. He decided to attack the embassy the following week believing that the same amount of people would be arriving early in the morning for work. What he didn't know was that almost the whole embassy had relocated up to Venice that weekend to work at the Summit, leaving only a skeleton staff at the embassy. Our bad guy assembled three homemade rockets and launchers in his hotel room, avoided the cleaning and hotel staff, put a timer on the device and set the rockets to fire at a little after 8:00 am one morning. He thought the area would be the busiest then based on his previous week's surveillance. He then departed Rome for parts unknown. We never did determine who or what his cause was. At the set time the rockets fired and flew over the busy Via Veneto and impacted just past the front gate in front of the security office. Fortunately the rockets were of the homemade variety and caused very little damage; a cracked bulletproof window to be exact and some stones kicked up against the building. No one was hurt or killed but the news of the attack traveled fast to both Washington and all the staff in Venice attending the Summit. This is where Leo, one of my assistants, comes into my story. Leo wasn't regarded as one of the super stars in Diplomatic Security but I can tell you he probably was one of its best investigators. Once he set his mind to the case, the end result was outstanding. So we have the rocket attack. Everyone, including my whole Security staff, with the exception of Leo, is up in Venice at the Summit. I call Leo, give him his marching orders and by the time I get back to Rome he has put together a complete report of the chain of events surrounding the bombing. I send off copies to our Washington Headquarters and even give our local FBI friends at the embassy a copy. The response from D.C. was "who did this fantastic report?" My response, "Leo." Their response, "You're shitting me!" My response, "I told you that Leo was a good Agent, you should have believed me."

After I later departed Rome, Leo began an extensive investigation into local corruption at the Embassy after he heard some rumors floating around. The thing about Leo was that once he got something in his head, there was no stopping him. Seems he heard somewhere that some of the locals in our General Services Office were getting kickbacks from contractors that they awarded work to. So Leo, being the good investigator that he was, starts to check this out. He snoops around the embassy, checks out a villa being built by the local head of our General Services Section and sees that the building was probably worth several million liras. Leo realizes that this guy don't get that much salary just working at the Embassy. So, after several weeks of intense investigation Leo has put the whole thing together, found out that several contractors getting work through the embassy were in fact building this villa for the head local in General Services and for little or no cost to him. So as the story goes, the evidence is presented to the appropriate people at the embassy, the GSO Head Local is fired and later is arrested by the Italian tax people for breaking some Italian laws too. So Leo comes out a hero and again proves to everyone that he is an expert investigator and someone you don't want checking you out.

Another major event took place while I was at Rome but I didn't become aware of it until a few years later when I got back to Washington. Eldridge Ames had been assigned to Rome about the same time as me and would later get arrested for spying for the Russians. Ames was with the CIA and although neither I, nor any of my assistants, remembered ever meeting or seeing him while in Rome, he was in fact there. After his arrest I received a telephone call from one of the major news agencies asking me to discuss Ames as he was there the same time as me. When I responded that I didn't know or ever meet Mr. Ames, the newsperson couldn't understand it since I was the Head of Security in Rome at the time. I then explained that there were several annex buildings in Rome besides the Embassy and over 400 American employees working there and so it was very unlikely that you ever got to know everyone.

The Ames story was interesting one to say the least and just recently one of the television networks ran a TV series called "Assets" which chronicled Ames and his spying and even included a small bit about Rome but nothing in any great detail.

Besides some of these security incidents during my stay in Rome there were even more dumb and funny things that took place while I were there. Our Ambassador was a great person and the embassy staff was continually invited to social and representational functions at his Residence. One of the big draws to these events, although it never happened that I am aware of, was the constant rumor that Cicciolina was going to attend an event. For those of you who have never heard of Cicciolina, she is a Hungarian born, Italian porn star, who in 1986 was elected to the Parliament in Italy. Every time the Ambassador hosted an event the rumors started to fly that she was invited and would be coming to it. This resulted in all the American staff, who might otherwise have sent their regrets to the Ambassador that they couldn't attend for some reason, to change their minds and attend, myself included. Everyone wanted to see Cicciolina in person but few ever did and as I said, I never heard of her actually coming to a function at the Ambassador's but he usually invited her.

While we're talking about porn stars, let me tell you about the Marine Ball in Rome one year. A friend of mine and a Security Officer at our embassy in China decided to attend. He had previously been considered for the RSO spot in Rome but that was before I forced my way into the position based on my seniority. He showed up at the Marine Ball in his Sunday best, tux and tie, along with chrome-plated dog tags around his neck (which we thought was a little strange, but to each his own) and a beautiful woman on his arm who would knock your socks off. When I said something to my local investigator about how beautiful she was, he started to laugh and said that this was one of Cicciolina's girl friends who made porno movies with her. No one could figure out how our friend had managed to get her as his date for the ball although our office spent many a day debating about it.

Then there was the time that Michael Jackson came to Rome for a concert and the Ambassador decided to have a large reception for Michael at the

Residence but he couldn't decide who to invite from our embassy and who not to invite. He really didn't want to hurt anyone's feelings so he decided that the best course of action was to not invite anyone from our embassy. That way no one would be slighted, just the whole embassy. I didn't care since as head of security I could always invite myself since my staff and I had to provide security and keep things safe. So Michael shows up in Rome, staying just across the street from our Embassy and makes a few solo appearances on his balcony which we manage to see from our office. The night of the big event arrives and Michael and his group show up at the Residence to meet the elite of Rome and its Diplomatic Corps. Unbeknownst to anyone, myself included, a few of the Marine Guards decide that it would be cool to crash the party, meet Michael Jackson and check things out. They even invited a visiting Seabee who was at the embassy doing some work for us. The Marines get all dressed up in their Sunday's finest and head off to the Residence. When they get to the entrance and the security checkpoint, the local guards know them and just assume they have been invited and so they are allowed in. The group then goes through an informal reception line and begins to mingle with the guests. They also avoid me and the rest of my security staff somehow. As the evening progresses the Ambassador finally spots them and asks his social secretary who is standing next to him, "Who are those guys as they really look familiar?" She responds, "Ya, they should look familiar, they're Marines at our embassy." This immediately puts the Ambassador into a mini-rage and he quietly goes over to the Marines and throws them out of his party. I never heard anything about it until the next day when both the Marine Gunny SGT. and I get a call from the Ambassador promptly at the start of business. We have no idea about what this is all about but we are to report to the Ambassador's Office immediately. When we get into his office he goes on to tell us the story and although laughing quite a bit, asks us how darn the Marines crash his party. He says he wants the Gunny and I to discipline these guys but good. He then adds that maybe it would be even better if we brought the guilty parties to his office and he can reprimand them instead. I quickly defuse this idea as I'm truly afraid that the Marines might begin to laugh or do something that would cause even more problems. I assure the Ambassador that the Gunny and I will ream their asses out appropriately, which we do while having a little bit of a laugh. You just have to love the Marines sometimes and some of the things they end up doing. As long as we're doing Marine stories I'll throw this one out before I finish up on the Michael Jackson visit. I get a call one morning in Rome from the Director of the U.S. Information Service, the old USIS, now called the Office of Diplomacy, and he asks me to come to his office, located on the compound as he has something to discuss with me. When I get there I see that his office is in a bit of disarray. His desk is a bit messed up and that there is an empty wine bottle lying on the floor next to it. He begins to piece together a story about how he suspects one of the Marines of having a small party with his girlfriend in his office the night before. The Director continues to explain how he further suspects that the Marine and his girlfriend may have had sex on his desk since there are several smudges on the desktop, some of which resembled someone's ass. So my job, should I decide to accept this assignment, is to find the culprit and bring him to justice and also back to the Director for some further ass reaming. You might think I'm making some of these Marine stories up but I assure you I am not. This case was never resolved although we had a few candidates.

Ok, back to the Michael Jackson saga. The day after the party at the Ambassador's, Michael has a concert in the near by soccer stadium and the Ambassador and one of the famous Italian designers, Valentino I think, decide to attend the concert along with the Ambassador's wife. So being a Michael Jackson fan at the time, I tell the Ambassador that I think I should accompany him to the concert in addition to the regular security team since there will be big crowds and the possibility of problems there. He readily agrees and off we go and naturally the seats are great and I am sitting right behind the Ambassador where I have a fantastic view of the stage and the show. Evidently both the Ambassador and Valentino weren't big Michael Jackson fans or didn't realize just how loud the concert could get as they sat through the entire concert with their fingers pushed into their ears to try to cut down on the noise. The concert finally ended, much to the pleasure of the Ambassador and Valentino and off we go to the Residence to drop off the Ambassador and his wife and end the night. Well, we do drop off Mrs. Ambassador, but the Ambassador then informs me that there is a big after party and we are going to that. We make our way there and it is a really up scale restaurant/club in the downtown area. As the Ambassador is getting out of the limo he tells me "Come on upstairs and party a little and have a good time." I reply, "Sure thing I'll be up there shortly." There is already a ton of security at this place and I seriously considering taking the Ambassador's up on his offer, however, I feel a bit underdressed compared to the beautiful people of Rome. I finally decide to just watch the goings-on from the limo and wait for the Ambassador. The Ambassador eventually returns and asks me if I had a good time upstairs. Dumb me, I reply " I didn't go up to the party." Whereupon he says, and I still remember it fairly well, "God Dam It! When I tell you to go have a good time I want you to listen to me and have a good time." Over and Out! What was I thinking to not go and have a good time? A good thing he didn't hold a grudge.

One of the cool things about being in Rome and being Catholic is the fact that the Diplomatic Corps gets special tickets to the Christmas and Easter Mass. The security office also became good friends with the Swiss Guards at The Vatican and so they allowed us to drive into the Vatican proper and park whenever we had a function to attend there. We reciprocated by making sure the guards were always invited to the events at the Marine House and at the Embassy. Both masses were really special and afforded you an upfront and close view not only of the mass but the Papa, as the Pope is affectionately called in Italy. Saint Peters is an old and historic building but does not have heat or AC and so when you attended midnight mass there on Christmas you had to be prepared to dress warmly and spend 4-5 hrs. in church. Mass got underway at Midnight but you were expected to be in your seats at least two hours before even though you have reserved seats. And no there were no choirs singing all this time as one might expect. The choir started up about five minutes before the service and before then you just sit in silence and contemplated Saint Peters and God. Once mass got underway the Pope made his entrance and everyone stood and applauded him as he moved toward the altar. The mass continued and lasted about 2 hours or so and finally after about 5 hrs. you were free to head home and go to bed. Easter mass is basically the same, however, that mass is held in Saint Peters Square and all the VIPs and Diplomatic Corps sat on the roof of The Vatican and watched the mass taking place below them. The only difference was that instead of freezing in Saint Peters Cathedral, you were roasting on its rooftop. I can remember several people passing out on the roof from the heat and long wait. Water and medical staff were usually stationed on the roof to assist any people with problems. Again it is about 5 hrs. from start to finish when attending Easter Mass.

One thing we used to laugh about at the embassy was how all the VIPs, Members of Congress, Senators, etc., came to Rome and wanted, and expected, a personal audience with the Pope. No matter what the embassy did, we could never get it across to them that yes this was the Pope, who just happened to be a Head of a Country, The Vatican. And NO you can't have a personal audience with him. Does everyone from overseas, who is not the Head of State, get a meeting with our President? I don't think so! So why do you think you should get a personal one on one meeting with the Pope? Many of our Senators and Members of Congress and VIPs who thought they were important, weren't that important when it came to meeting the Pope. That's why he did his weekly General Audiences so that you and the common man can see him and get his Papal blessing. You can ever buy a pair of rosary beads blessed by the Pope for a small fee.

One thing I forgot to mention at the start of my Rome stories was that we arrived in Rome about a week or so before August, or Ferragosto as it is known in Italian. We were told that many of the local businesses, stores and restaurants were closed in August but we were in for a big surprise when Ferragosto finally arrived. The first weekend in August arrived and Pat and I decided to take Scooter, our Afghan Hound, for a walk along the Via Veneto and maybe catch a coffee somewhere. When we finally got onto the Via Veneto it was totally deserted. I mean no one and no traffic was in sight. Just about every store, shop and restaurant was not only closed but shuttered so that you couldn't even tell what kind of business establishment it was. I am NOT kidding you, Pat and I thought they had either evacuated the city or the bomb had dropped while we were sleeping; that is how empty and deserted Rome's downtown was. At night we wondered the empty streets and most times managed to find a lone restaurant open so that we could get something to eat. One restaurant we found opened was Mariano Restaurante, no relation to me, and when we informed the staff at the restaurant of my name they didn't seem impressed as I think they believed I was trying to get a free meal out of them. In checking the Internet I see that Marianos has changed ownership and is now called Sapori Sardi, although several people did mention that they had been at the old Marianos. Even the embassy emptied out as everyone took off all of August or at least a good part of it. The other interesting thing about

Ferragosto was that the traffic along the main highways in Italy all headed south to such places as Naples, Sorrento, Pompeii, Capri and the Amalfi Coast. Traffic was terrible, driving was fast and reckless, and the drivers from Europe, and especially Germany, liked to travel at high rates of speed despite that fact that the speed limit then was only 100 kmh or about 65 mph. One August there were over 350 people killed on the road between Rome and southern Italy. This is a land area smaller than New Jersey. The following year the Italians decided that they had to do something to decease the amount of fatalities on their roads during August. They decided to set up speed traps (especially at the border with Germany) and enforce the 100 kmh speed limit. On the first day that it was in place they issued over 400 traffic tickets, mostly to the Germans. The Germans and the German Government were infuriated to the extent that the Germans threatened to break off relations with the Italians if they didn't cease and desist with this stupid traffic law immediately. The Italians responded by saying that this was the posted speed limit, so obey it. Not sure how this finally washed out but it did come to a boiling point that August. Speaking of driving, driving in Rome and on the roadways around Rome was fast and furious. Pass whoever you can and get out front and stay there. If you couldn't find a regular parking space, just pull up on the sidewalk and park. If you're going to the grocery store or bakery and there's no parking spaces, just leave your car in the middle of the street and go do your shopping. So what if there was a line of cars backed up when you finished and they were blowing their horns at you and cursing you as you shopped. Give them a vulgar gesture in return and just get in your car and leave. It was unreal and funny when you saw it and you can never explain to the average person in the U.S. just how screwed up it was.

It didn't snow in Rome very often but when it did it was a hoot to watch the Italians try to drive in it. The snow didn't appear to phase them and they attempted to go as fast in the snow as when the streets were dry. One of our favorite pastimes when it snowed was to go out by one of the steep hills by our apartment and watch the Italians try to negotiate the hill either going up or down. Great entertainment!

Eating in Italy was a taste treat and I don't think we ever had a bad meal while we were stationed there. Expensive? YES! Bad tasting? NO!

Shopping was something different too as there weren't many supermarkets when we lived in Rome. Shopping was done at individual shops; the butcher, the baker, the vegetable stall, etc. Saturday was usually our grocery shopping day and it was at least a half day affair by the time we bought everything and then stopped at our favorite local restaurant for some vino and food. By the time we got home and unpacked everything, it was time to take a nap. Our lunch routine on shopping day also changed as we were in Rome for a while. First it was just a glass or two of wine with lunch, then half a carafe and finally a whole carafe. What the hell!

It was also funny to watch Italian women shop during the winter months as everyone tended to wear long fur coats while doing their Saturday chores. Naturally most of the wives at the Embassy ended up getting fur coats while in Rome. The embassy had some good contacts and so the coats were a good buy for us and greatly discounted for diplomats.

As I mentioned, our office covered all the diplomatic facilities in Italy, to include The Vatican and on the Island of Malta. Once we closed the security office at The Vatican I went there more often and took care of security problems and issues with our Ambassador. We also had a second Ambassador in Rome at FODAG, the U.S. Food and Agriculture Organization. Getting back to The Vatican. Most of the appointments to this posting were political and most of the Ambassador's also had lots of money to go with this posting. When eventually one of our Career Diplomats arrived to take over The Vatican he got a rude awakening when he found out that most of the previous Ambassadors had brought over not only all the furniture for their residences but also most of it for the office. So when our Career Diplomat arrived and started trying to find furnishings, there wasn't a lot to be had, much to his dismay. The other thing that materialized was that the current Residence for the Ambassador had been picked out by a predecessor who never spent the winter months in Italy. Since the house was mainly empty during the cold part of the year, no one realized that the only source of heat for this old residence were the fire places that were located in each and every room. Obviously the new Ambassador didn't want to have to attend to fires in each and every room during the winter in order to keep warm, but as it stood, there was no other source of heating currently in his house.   What was equally very interesting was that the Deputy Chief of Mission had a huge villa sitting on top of one of the highest hills by The Vatican with expansive grounds and a panoramic view of all of Rome. The DCM's house made the Ambassador's house look sick. Since the current DCM still had some time left on his assignment at The Vatican it would have been very awkward for the new Ambassador to bounce the DCM from his luxury digs.

We also had security responsibility for our embassy on the Island of Malta, which was a relatively quiet post from a security standpoint although there have since been some instances of terrorist incidents taking place there including the landing of an airliner that was hijacked by members of Abu Nidal in 1985. Malta is a pleasant mix of Europe and the Middle East, which is reflected in its history and its language. The Knights of Malta date back to the 1530s and the Order still exists today with over 11,000 knights worldwide. The language in Malta is Maltese, a combination of Italian and Arabic. I remember the first time I visited Malta I thought I was hearing Italian, when all of a sudden the words seemed to change and it began to sound like the person was speaking Arabic. The old sections of Malta reflect a Middle Eastern flavor in both architecture and the goods sold there. It was a quiet little island that most people have never visited or even heard of.

One last quick story about driving in Rome and car insurance. One afternoon I was out in the alley loading Scooter, our Afghan, into the back of the Alfa Romero that we used for trips outside of Rome, reserving the old Lancia for our everyday driving. The back door was open and as I'm putting Scooter into the back seat a car comes screaming up the alley and I hear a thump type sound. At first I wasn't sure what it was but quickly found out that the passing car had hit my back door, almost ripping it off the hinges. The car did finally stop and I ran over to it and begin to ask the rider what the hell he was thinking. Another inch or so and I would have been part of the door. After a little, well maybe a lot, of screaming the driver decides that I am a crazy person and he drives off. I ran after him and saw that he lived just down the alley and when I try to get him out of his house, he tries to fake not being home. I then decided to call my head investigator and have him come over along with some of my police friends. The nice thing about being in security is that we work daily with the police. They went to the guy's house and put the fear of God into him and he agreed to come up with the insurance to cover the damage. At the time I was getting ready to leave Rome in just a few months and so I had to get the Alfa fixed right away, since I'm sure the insurance money will be coming shortly. WRONG! In Italy, even though you pay much more for insurance than back in the states, the insurance companies negotiate your payment. Oh, your claim is 10,000 liras, how about we give you 4,000 liras right now and call it square? No! OK, we'll be in touch. A month later, how about 4,500 liras? No! OK, we'll be in touch. This can go on for well over a year and eventually they just wear you down and you end up settling for much less than the amount of your claim and your damages. Can you imagine if the insurance companies in the U.S. tried to pull this. There would be a riot.

Finally after two years, going on three, it was transfer time again and one of my old bosses requested that I join him back in Washington to head Diplomatic Security's Physical Security Division as its Director. The office was responsible for the physical security of all our diplomatic facilities throughout the world and would eventually become the government leader in the development of security products and standards used to protect our embassies overseas and government facilities in the United States. Several of the products developed by us would later be adopted by other elements of the Federal Government and some foreign governments to protect their embassies and facilities. So off to Washington, DC, for my final years with DS.

PSD-THE PHYSICAL SECURITY
DIVISION

Pat and I got back to the good old U.S.A. and had previously bought a house in Reston, Virginia, and so we're ready for our Washington tour and probably my last assignment with the State Department. Back in those days you had two options when you got to the senior levels in the Department. You could stay in your current pay grade and keep working until the mandatory retirement age, which I think back then was 60 years of age. Your second option electing to enter the Senior Service and go through five promotion panels and if, at the conclusion of the fifth or sixth panel you did not get promoted into the Senior Service you were mandatorily retired by the Department, however, the very next day you began to receive your retirement pension, regardless of your age and no matter how many years you had worked with the Department of State. I decided to go for option number Two. At that time we only had one promotion to the Senior Service in the Security element, and in most years None. There were 50 or so Special

177

Agents in competition for that coveted promotion. Needless to say I Did Not get promoted during my promotion window, I did Not Pass Go and was separated from the State Department, although after some fan fare and celebration and I did begin to collect my pension the very next month. How bad is that? I don't want to tell you what year this all happened to me as I don't want to date myself.

The Physical Security Programs Division was one of the largest Divisions that Diplomatic Security had at the time and I think my staff numbered about 40 or so contractors, Special Agents and Security Engineers. We worked closely with the Office of Foreign Buildings (FBO then, OBO now), who was responsible for carrying out our recommendations concerning physical security at new Embassies and for retrofitting existing facilities around the world. Every embassy overseas usually had a DS Security Officer assigned to it by the time I took over PSD. The days of the truly Regional Security Officer were long gone as DS at one point decided that any embassy or diplomatic facility with over 10 Americans merited a permanent RSO. I'm not sure I agree with this policy, however, it did help DS get some much needed personnel and eventually our organization grew from 300 or so Special Agents when I first joined DS in 1972 to almost 2,000 Agents, a figure that is still close to our current manpower. My office was a bit unusual when it came to funding projects since PSD decided what upgrades we should be doing overseas at our facilities but the purse strings with all the money rested with FBO. Whenever we wanted to do something, we had to convince them that this money would be well spent but they still had the final say as to whether the proposed project would go forward. Many of the projects did get the green light but an equal number got axed or postponed to what we called "out years" for future funding. Besides doing actual building projects we formulated the policies and procedures regarding the physical security standards required at all US diplomatic facilities throughout the world. We worked with other elements of the U.S. Government in establishing threat levels for every country overseas and then when this was finally approved government wide, we began to formulate physical security standards for all our facilities based upon the threat in a particular country. This entailed a lot of work and effort on the part of my staff but when we finally got the job done we had something that everyone was very proud of and which we felt would help to protect our facilities and people overseas.

The next step in the process was to begin to formulate what kinds of security equipment should be used to provide the levels of protection we desired. We worked with a large number of companies in the private sector in developing new products and improving existing ones so that we could meet the standards we had set. We helped developed windows and doors that could withstand up to 60 minutes of forced entry attack and were able to defeat ballistic attacks from weapons up to NATO type rounds. We found and helped to improve new types of heavy duty entry gates and barriers that could stop a 5 ton truck traveling at 50 miles an hour. We found window films that could contain the glass shards from a bomb explosion. After these items had been developed by various outside companies, we set up an extensive testing process whereby all items, before being accepted onto our vendors list, had to be tested at a private testing facility.The products would only be accepted by us for use overseas after they were certified by this testing facility that they could do what the manufacturer said they could and that the item met the degree of protection that we wanted. The result was a wide array of security equipment that we were confident could stand up to the threat that exited against our facilities overseas. This equipment has been tried and tested during a number of terrorist attacks at our facilities and I am happy to say that it met the challenge. Here's a quick story about our Embassy in Kuwait. After the first Gulf War our military went back into Kuwait with one of my people from PSD to check the embassy out and reopen it as it had been completely evacuated during the conflict. Our group got to the Embassy building entrance and everyone realized that no one had keys to get back into the Chancery. One of the military types says no problem, "we'll just breach the entrance door." In order words, we'll open it with a small explosive charge. So they put the charge on the door and blow it, however, they failed to get the door open as it is one of our 60 minute forced entry doors. At the time we did teach certain elements of the military how to get by our door systems in the event they had to get in during a crises or emergency. This group however, wasn't one of them. The military guys decided to give it one more try and again were unsuccessful in gaining entry. They finally ended up blowing a hole through the wall with a shape charge and eventually got in. Our high standards and tested equipment eventually became the norm for use by the entire Federal Government and is used both overseas and domestically to meet the terrorist threats that exist in the world today.

As Director I got to visit a number of facilities that were attacked by terrorists over the 5-6 years in PSD. We went to these sites to see what worked and what didn't. We also wanted to see the extent of damage and study the methods used by terrorist groups so that we could establish countermeasures against future attacks. The other thing that began to develop during my stay in PSD was how terrorists began to change their methods of operation. When I first went to work for the Department of State the types of threats were much different from when I led PSD or from how they are today. Back in the 70's and 80's you had your typical mass demonstrations, some of which got out of hand when groups would converge on our Embassies and attack them. You had the threat of a lone assassin attacking and trying to kill the Ambassador or some other diplomat. You had letter and package bombs being sent to our embassies overseas or the small bomb being thrown over the wall at an embassy. The degree and level of sophistication that would eventually develop for these attacks, and the way terrorist carried out their attacks, would later require us to reexamine our standards and types of equipment we used in order to meet the current and new threats which faced us. Back then we only envisioned a chemical, biological or radiological type attack as something that was very unlikely to happen. Now these types of attacks are on the top of security's list of what to look out for in the months and years to come.

Terrorists would eventually develop well coordinated and sophisticated types of attacks on our overseas facilities and the amounts of explosives used in these attacks would grow and grow until they were using thousands of kilos of explosive materials that could product massive explosions and after pressures and result in mass destruction and casualties.

At the end of my book I'll talk briefly about some of my assignments as a WAE, rehired annuitant, after I finally did retire from State Department. As I mentioned, the types of threats increased beyond what we initially envisioned. Terrorists were now loading vehicles with large amounts of explosives and causing mass destruction and casualties overseas. Suicide bombers became popular and were highly successful in targeting VIPs. Eventually we would see 9/11 where terrorists would use commercial aircraft to take down the World Trade Center in NYC. We had thought about this threat even back when I was in PSD but never on the scale and degree of coordination that we saw during the 9/11 attacks. A number of years before 9/11 a young man managed to fly a small aircraft, avoiding radar detection, and land at Red Square in Moscow. We always felt that this was a very viable means for attacking embassies overseas and I believe it still is, given the large number of private aircraft owned throughout the world. We never, however, focused on using large commercial airliners to do this type of attack.

Eventually the Internet would appear with its many resources and both law enforcement and terrorists would have a new tool to greatly assist them. Terrorists could find bomb making instructions on line, they could communicate with each other via websites and e-mail, they could use Google Earth to see facilities across the world that might be a possible target and never have to leave their safe havens. This was witnessed just recently as I wrote this book when terrorist killed a journalist by beheading him and then posted it on YouTube. In present days, terrorists can record their attacks and assassinations and put them on YouTube for the world to see. The Internet would become both a blessing and a curse for security experts because it could both aid them but also provided vast resources for the terrorists to use in their attacks on us too. The last time I did an ATA course overseas for Police I told them that an old manual, circa 60's-70's, The Weatherman's Cookbook, was still available on the Internet as a pdf download and you could even buy a Hard Covered copy of it from a book store in London. This book told you how to assemble bombs, make ingredients for bombs and all sorts of other bad ways to terrorize people or just bust your boss's balls. That was over 40 years ago and it is still out there if you want it.

PSD initially helped to fund the particle trace detector that you see nowadays at almost everything airport throughout the world. We originally worked with a technology firm in Massachusetts on this device and the first device was manufactured it looked like a gigantic ice cream cart. It was about 5-6' long, 3-4'high and about 3' wide. It used a Black & Decker dust buster to suck air particulars from the air and then a computer analyzed all the particle matter to see if there was any explosive material present. It worked OK but environmental conditions sometimes played havoc on the machine. When I got assigned to Rome, the Director of PSD in Washington asked me if I'd like to get a prototype and test it in Rome. I said, "Why Not!" What I didn't realize was that the dust, dirt and air pollution in Rome would quickly clog everything on the device and make it completely worthless. Eventually the technology would be further developed, the size of the device would be shrunk down so that it could fit on a table top and it would be used world wide, not only at our embassies, but at almost every airport in the world to check items and determine if any type of explosive materials were present in the item or if the items had even come in contact with certain elements that could pose a threat.

We worked with a number of laboratories and universities to develop products and computer programs to help us determine the impact of explosives on various types of facilities based on the amount of explosives used and the standoff distances in place. We got together with Sandia National Laboratories in New Mexico to develop security products that might be useful in our battle against terrorism. Sandia's web site gives the following info. concerning what they currently do. "For more than 60 years, Sandia has delivered essential science and technology to resolve the nation's most challenging security issues. Sandia

National Laboratories is operated and managed by Sandia Corporation, a wholly owned subsidiary of Lockheed Martin Corporation. Sandia Corporation operates Sandia National Laboratories as a contractor for the U.S. Department of Energy's National Nuclear Security Administration (NNSA) and supports numerous federal, state, and local government agencies, companies, and organizations." Sandia National Laboratories is a self-sufficient facility that generates its own income flow to maintain their operations. During the Cold War Sandia had no trouble finding customers to serve and generate income for them. When the Cold War ended Sandia had to scramble to find services that other types of consumers were interested in. State Department and my office employed their services to come up with new and ingenious ideas for denying access to our facilities and devices we could use should a crowd converge on an embassy and try to force their way into the building. They also worked on robotics and during one demonstration I attended they had a remote controlled vehicle that could be used to do patrols and even use deadly force to neutralize a threat. I must say I really enjoyed my visits to Sandia as they could sometimes come up with products and presentations that you sometimes thought were only in the realm of science fiction.

PSD also had the final say in the design of all our new embassies that were being erected overseas. The engineering security officers and contractors that worked for me would follow an embassy's construction from start to finish. We looked at the initial blueprints and designs to make sure the building was being built according to standards we had formulated and that the security equipment being used had all been certified according to our test standards. We visited the sites of the embassy so that we could see things up close and personal and made sure that standoff distances were being adhered to, or if they weren't, we came up with some new type of equipment to handle the threat in that particular country. When the building was finally ready for occupancy we traveled out to do a final punch list and made sure that all our standards were adhered to and that the builders didn't cut costs on anything. All embassy buildings had to pass this final muster before our employees could finally move in. All our facilities had to be approved up the chain of command from my office and up through the Undersecretary and finally Congress. Sometimes when certain standards and criteria couldn't be met, a waiver package had to be prepared for approval up through the chain of command. One of the biggest problems we frequently encountered were our setback standards, which I think at the time were about 100' or more on all sides. Our government usually received the parcels of land for our embassies from the Host Government and sometimes large land parcels just aren't available. In these instances we would do a waiver, however, there was many a time when my office, PSD, did up the waiver package and recommended to our management that these waivers should not be approved for one reason or another. We presented the pros and cons of the waiver and many times upper management just rolled us and the waiver went forward despite our objections. This tended to irritate us but at least we had a piece of paper in hand that had our objection recorded so that if anything bad happened in the future we could pull the paper out and tell everyone "See, we told you so!"

So after 6 years directing PSD it was finally time to be "selected out" or in none government vernacular, retire and head out to greener pastures. The big question was "Was I really leaving Uncle Sam once and for all?"

LIFE IN THE ACADEMIC WORLD

Right before I was ready to retire I was contacted by a security consultant who was doing some work at Yale University in New Haven, CT, and who was also helping them to recruit a new physical security director for their campus after a student was killed at the university. "Say, wasn't that what I had been doing for almost 20 years? and was I interested in the job?" After a quick interview, panel selection by several Yale officers, I got ready to join the academic world after just retiring from State. I am not going to get too involved in talking about my time there except to say that I did get a lot of worthwhile physical security projects completed in my 2 years plus although it was often a very frustrating two years. For any of you previously or currently employed by the U.S. Government, believe me, the bureaucratic red tape you may encounter working for Uncle Sam is nothing compared to trying to work in the world of academia. As you are trying to get things done, there are TWO things you always dreaded to hear. The first."That sounds like a good idea but let's form a committee and discuss things further." That is when a group gets formed from various elements of the University and eventually the people on this committee, no matter what their backgrounds or offices are at the university, all of a sudden become Security Experts! I remember one meeting where I was proposing a project for consideration and approval, when all of a sudden a woman says" Well, I was talking with the janitor and he said, blah, blah, blah." Well, I didn't realize the janitor was a security expert. Once things got into a Committee, you could forget about ever getting much done on that project in "Your Lifetime". I think academic folks just wanted committees to go on ad nauseam so that every Tuesday or Wednesday, at 2 p.m., they had something to do.

The second Kiss of Death, especially if you are at Yale sounded like this. Well, "Why don't you see what they are doing at Harvard and Princeton on that!" Well, OK, but do you realize that Harvard and Princeton aren't remotely similar to Yale in geographics or demographics? Yale is surrounded by low income housing and when I was there, the downtown area of New Haven was rundown and most businesses were either closed or closing since even Yale couldn't support them. Now let's venture up to Harvard and Princeton and see those nice bistro restaurants, a thriving downtown area and no beggars along the streets, like at Yale.

The Secretary of the University once asked me how to get rid of beggars and panhandlers on the streets and sidewalks at Yale. I replied, "tell the students to stop giving them $5-$10 whenever they see them." Hell, when a panhandler can make $100 a day on the street to buy some good cheap vino why on earth would he not continue to hang around the University? One time Yale decided that they would try giving the panhandlers chits so that these starving people could get some good wholesome foods at one of the few restaurants still open downtown. Well, that went over BIG! Most of the street people looked at the chit and threw it on the ground when a student gave them one. Hey! you can't get wine with this! Just give me a buck! So this program failed shortly after it got going.

Enough of Yale and my frustrations while working there. After about 2 years or so I decided that enough was enough and that if they didn't want to listen to some constructive advise on how to improve their security I might as well leave and do something else. So I quit. I sent the President of the University a brief e-mail telling him that eventually someone else was going to get killed at Yale because the current administration was not very responsive to security needs and that it was just a matter of time.

So Pat and I decided to leave Connecticut and move to Myrtle Beach, SC, as we had gotten into golf while at Yale, since they do have a fantastic golf course where the staff can play and that is not open to the general public. Would we like MB? Who knew back then but it was someplace to go and definitely better than Connecticut with its high taxes. We moved to MB and now I had to decide if I should be retired/retired or do something else. Fun wise, we got into golf at Prestwick

CC,where we ended up moving and had a Pete Dye Golf Course to keep us entertained for years to come. A quick note. Pete Dye Golf Courses NEVER get easier the more you play them. I had gotten certified as an Open Water Diver after taking some lessons while we were still in Rome, Italy and heading down to Sardinia and Club Med. When I got to Myrtle Beach I decided to take more dive courses and thanks to Joe, my instructor, eventually got to the Asst. Instructor level and now spend many a summer day working on a local dive boat and having a good old time. This was all great, however, it didn't bring in any additional coin into the house besides my State Department pension. So I decided to become a WAE at State Department. That's a "When Actually Employed" person who is someone who remains on the U.S. Department of State's employee roles but only gets paid when he actually works and goes somewhere.

Diplomatic Security had the foresight to keep former employees on the roles since they were mostly senior Special Agents who had gone around the block and could readily fill in at embassies around the world whenever a need arose.

So I began my second career as a WAE with the U.S. Department of State. Remember my last chapter when I said, Am I really done with the U.S Government and the Department of State. So now I can say, "No." So for the next 20 years or so, in fact until the present time, I became a WAE, When Actually Employed, for DS and the Department of State. I'm not going to go into each and every assignment that I have done for DS over the past years and months but I do have some interesting and quick stories to add before finishing my book.

LIFE AS A RETIRED SPECIAL AGENT

There are two nice things about being a WAE for the State Department. The first is that no matter how bad a post is that you're going to, You're only there for a short time! Maybe a month or two and then you're out of there and can say to yourself, "Thank God I wasn't assigned there when I was working full time. Two-three years there, Holy Shit!" The fact is that even the crappy posts have many pluses to them but I'm still glad I managed to avoid them during my first career. The next good thing about WAE assignments are, "You DON'T have to do them if you don't want to." You bid on assignments and if you get it, Great. If you don't you continue to do your thing at home; golf, dive, whatever turns you on. State Department is one of the few U.S. Government agencies that realized the vast assets they had and how to use them long after a person retired. Other law enforcement agencies have seen what DS does and begun to explore doing the same thing with some of their veterans.

So here's a few short stories about some

of the TDYs I did for DS and the U.S. Department of State.

1997: Lusaka, Zambia: Lusaka was a sleepy little town and nothing much usually happened there, however, while I was there the host government decided to burn down a number of shanty type shops that were in the downtown area. It seems that the government had just built a new and smart looking mall type building and they wanted the locals to house their daily market there. Oh yes, and they also wanted them to pay some rent too. So one evening the old market mysteriously burnt to the ground, pissing off all the merchants and causing wide spread demonstrations and riots throughout the town. Police quickly moved in with troops and tear gas and the mob responded by burning down the Defense Ministry that was just down the street from our Embassy. All the mass marches came up a street right next to our embassy as they headed to the government buildings to protest. So there I stand watching the demonstrators come by and making sure the guards and Marines are all alert in case the crowd decides to make a quick stop at our embassy. Out comes our Ambassador and proceeds to get into her car and is preparing to depart the embassy compound. I ask her just where she plans to go? In case she hasn't heard, the city is in dishevel and there are riots all over the place. She replies,"Well that is exactly where I'm headed. The people here all know me and Love me and so I'm going to go down to where the demonstrations are and tell those folks, "Now you just stop this!!!" My mouth fell open as I couldn't believe what she had just said. I firmly tell her that as RSO, "I would Strongly Recommend Against This!" Whereupon she closes her car door and off she goes, hopefully to be seen again. Yes, she did return unharmed although what just happened is something typical of many of our Ambassadors. They truly believe that all the local people know and love them and that everyone is their friend. I wish this were so but we have lost our fair share of Ambassadors to unstable people and terrorists over the years. The recent events in Syria are but an example of this. I am confident that at some point our security folks told our Ambassador that Benghazi was too dangerous to go to but as we have seen, he went there and the results were disastrous. I should add that this is solely my opinion based on working overseas for many years.

1998: Tokyo, Japan: An uneventful TDY although my arrival came on the wings of the sarin gas attack on the Tokyo Subway system and so people were a little on end because of that. I quickly found out that you better speak Japanese if you want to do anything or planned on eating there. Most restaurants didn't have English-speaking waiters but fortunately most restaurants did have models of various food dishes on display and so you were challenged to examine the model and try to figure out just what the hell it was. You had a 50/50 chance that if you ordered it, it would be something that you truly wanted to eat. I finally found one place where a girl spoke English and so I became a regular there. Also watched a lot of sumo wresting as that was about all I could find on local TV that was worth watching. We even had a few minor earthquakes which scared the shit out of me but when I went outside although I was the only one that appeared to be concerned.

195

There was also the geisha house just outside the back gate of the US housing compound. It was really something although I did not frequent it not because of desire but because of money. The geishas would come down the alley daily around 4:00 P.M. fully clothes in their silk kimonos and pancake makeup and little wooden shoes. Later their clients would begin to arrive in their Mercedes, BMWs and even a Rolls Royce or two. Big bucks for this place and I understand they were not prostitutes but rather did traditional ceremonies like the tea service, danced or sang while that their Japanese clientele looked on.

Then there was the yearly St. Pat's party sponsored by all the law enforcement agencies at the embassy and attended by all their counterparts in Japanese law enforcement. LOTS and LOTS of booze flowed down the throats of everyone that night but especially the Japanese law officers. Hell, free booze and expensive liquor to boot. Later in the night the old Karaoke machine and TV got cranking and things really got nuts. The Japanese love Karaoke and everyone got singing and drinking until there wasn't anything left to drink. The party finally ended and everyone who could still walk began to leave. Those who couldn't walk were assisted down to the back alley where we summoned a taxi for our comrades after firmly propping them against a building so they wouldn't fall on their asses. Happy St. Patty's Day!

1998: Nairobi, Kenya: When I arrived in Kenya and was briefed by the Embassy everyone said to just worry about the crime as there was no terrorist threat there. We'll see how this advice turned out to be wrong. Crime was out of sight however in Nairobi. The week before I arrived a young child was caught by a crowd for stealing from someone and the crowd beat the poor kid to death and left him lying on the roadway right in front of our Embassy. On another occasion one of our employees was on his way back from lunch when 5 youths attacked and beat him in broad daylight and on a public sidewalk just down the street from our Embassy. Each youth grabbed an arm or leg and the fifth person knocked him to the ground and then they went on to beat and rob him. He said that persons walking down the sidewalk merely looked at the scene and kept walking. No one made any effort to help him. I should add that his guy was an African American about 6' and 230 lbs. and looked like a fullback for the NFL. Another day one of our employees was having his car checked at the security checkpoint right in front of our embassy when a guy runs up, opens the car door, grabs his briefcase and hauls ass down the street, while 3 of our guards and 3 police officers stand there looking dumbfounded. The apartment I stayed at for about six weeks was on a compound with guards, a high fence with a 220v. electric wire running along the top of it and we had a rapid response force in case of an emergency. I know the wire on top was hot as one night a truck hit a lamp pole and the pole came down on the electric wire and suddenly all the lights in the compound went out and sparks were flying. At first I thought we had been attacked and grabbed my gun, which I faithfully carried in Kenya, and headed to the front gate were I got the full story of the truck accident. The rapid response team I mentioned consisted of a flatbed truck with two benches and 10 of the biggest Africans you could imagine with football helmets on and carrying large clubs that would be used to beat the hell out of any unfortunate robber that got caught on one of our housing compounds. Unfortunately, the robbers had it down to a science and knew they had about 1-2 minutes to get in and out of a house before these guys showed up. If they were unlucky enough that the truck was very close when the alarm sounded, they were in for a big surprise. The entrance to my apartment building had a steel grate door to get in, my front door had a steel grate door in front of it, the entry to my bedroom area had a steel grate door, all the windows were barred, the house was alarmed, I had an emergency radio and panic alarm in the bedroom, and I still slept with a gun on the night stand next to my bed. These robbers didn't care, they still tried to get into embassy apartments. They must have had a death wish! People in the United States don't appreciate how safe they are when you compare the U.S. to some of the countries that I've visited over the years.

Other than some of the crime I just mentioned it was a fairly quiet time in Kenya. In talks with our Ambassador she continually told me that our Embassy should be moved because it was right out on the street and on one of the busiest corners in downtown Nairobi and was in danger. I totally agreed with her and promised to talk with folks when I got back to Washington. It would turn out that both she and I were correct, our embassy shouldn't have been where it was. Less than a week after I got home from this assignment I heard the news that two of our embassies overseas, one in Kenya and the other in Tanzania, had been bombed. At first I thought it was probably just a small bomb or something minor but when I finally got the full story and saw the coverage on TV I saw that both embassies had been destroyed and that several people had been killed and hundreds wounded. I couldn't believe that I had been there less than a week before and that if the terrorists had attacked a week earlier I would have been there and perhaps even been one of the dead. When the list of those killed came out for Nairobi I felt especially sad and on the verge of tears. Among those killed was a young Marine who had just made Sergeant and whose wet down promotion party I had attended; a young U.S. Army officer from the Defense Attaché's Office who had just arrived that month and who had taken a day off to show me around town and drive me through a wild game park just on the outskirts of town; The Consul General and his son who I had just played a few rounds of golf with in Nairobi and the General Services Officer who I worked while setting up the Fourth of July party at the Ambassador's residence. There were others plus scores of Kenyans who were injured or blinded by the blast. Many of the injured were in a glass fronted building directly behind our embassy where the bomb exploded. The one plus thing regarding the bombing was that the local guards did what they were trained to do and didn't allow the vehicle to drive down into the underground garage at our Embassy, where the damage would have been even worse. I still think back to this event and wonder if there was more that could have been done to prevent it. The security there was sufficient given the threat that existed at the time. Eventually the Ambassador would get her wish and we would get a new and security improved embassy outside of town but not before many lives were lost.

Nicholas Mariano

1999: Shanghai, People's Republic of China: When I arrived in Shanghai I was amazed by the mass of humanity in that town. Some say Calcutta is mobbed, however, Shanghai has many more people, cars and people on bicycles, as that is one the main means of transportation for the masses. Crossing streets there, ever with traffic lights, took several tries as you had to either avoid car traffic or on the next light, the heavy bike traffic. It could sometimes take a few minutes to get across some of the main and heavier trafficked streets. I was put up at the beautiful Portman Hotel. Right next to it they were constructing what was at the time the tallest building in the world. The footprint for the building was mammoth and it went down and down below the street level. They were also building everywhere throughout the city and there were construction cranes along the horizon for as far as the eye could see. One person at the Consulate told me that over 75% of the construction cranes in the world were in Shanghai at the time. Next door to the Portman was a Hard Rock Cafe and at night, along with 2 for 1 drinks, some of the most beautiful women you have ever seen were there eating. When I mentioned this to someone at the Consulate they told me at all the prostitutes had a snack there at night before hitting the streets. I also found out that prostitution was very, very, illegal in China although it was still a very active trade. Penalty for being caught with a prostitute was several years of Hard Labor in a Chinese prison.

A funny thing did happen at the Consulate one night and went unexplained by us, however, we did have our theories. The Consulate was having a complete refurbishing and some of the areas that were formerly the

Consul General's living space were being converted back to office areas. There was a 24 hr. Marine Security Guard at the Consulate and one night while he was making his rounds of the second floor he turned to discover a Chinese person out on the ledge outside a window and who appeared quite startled to see the Marine looking at him. The Marine also was quite startled but did sound the alarm and recalled the rest of the Marine Security Guard Detachment back to the Consulate. A thorough search of the building and grounds failed to uncover the intruder. Neither our local guards inside the compound nor the Chinese PAP Guards on the outside perimeter admitted to seeing anything unusual or any persons roaming the grounds. Eventually the incident was reported back to Washington but where the ledge man had vanished to was unknown. I should add as a quick note that also next to the Consulate was a building, not one of ours, that had a mysterious airshaft on it facing our compound. No one could figure out the reason for such a large airshaft but several of us had our theories about it.

1999: Beijing, People's Republic of China: The embassy there was fairly old and reminded me of the design used at many U.S. Post Offices. In other words, it was one Ugly Looking Embassy. I am happy to say that a new Embassy has since been built. Anyway, my big pass time while in Beijing was eating out as prices were cheap to say the least. The Marines at our embassy and the Chinese PAP Guards assigned to the embassy exterior were good Informal friends who occasionally gave each other a wave when no one was watching. Tuesday nights I went to another agent's apartment and we watched Monday Night Football from the USA that was broadcast in

Japanese. It was something to try to follow what was happening but at least we could watch the games while we feasted on an assortment of Chinese takeout. Nothing much happened during my TDY although things got exciting about a week after I left. NATO forces attacked sites in Belgrade and it just so happened that the Chinese Embassy was hit and some of its staff were injured and killed. Mass protests took place outside U.S. facilities throughout the world, since the plane responsible for the attack was U.S. Fighter jet. The staff at our embassy in Beijing was kept captive at the embassy compound for a number of days by mass crowds that had positioned themselves outside the gates. What made this a bit comical to me was watching the Nighty News and having the reporter say how bad things were getting there as no food was allowed to enter the compound and what would the poor Americans eat. Well, a little secret. The embassy had a full mini-super market on compound, along with a large restaurant for the staff. Hell, they had enough food between the two facilities to last it out for a few weeks. No one was going to starve to death like the news was reporting. But it made the event all the more exciting.

2000: Colombo, Sri Lanka: Colombo had been one of my countries of responsibility when I was assigned to New Delhi, India. The country had been ravished by several years of civil war between the Tamil Liberation Group and the Government of Sri Lanka. When I arrived there for a TDY it was a completely changed city. No tourists frequented the many ocean front hotels and military checkpoints were found all over the city and on the major roadways, especially between Colombo and it's international airport. A new Embassy had since been built and the President of the country lived just down from our Embassy adding to the security problems of the Embassy. Fortunately nothing happened during this TDY and I soon returned home to Washington only to find out that there was going to be another TDY to Colombo in a month or so. So I figured, what the hell, nice place, nice hotel apartment to live in and a little extra money. About two months later I again headed to Colombo. When I got back to the Embassy I saw that part of the roof was covered with a blue tarp. I come to find out that between my first departure from Colombo and my return, part of the roof fell off the Chancery Building. Now this was a fairly new building and the roof consisted of earthen tiles that were fastened with some sort of nail set up. What appeared to have happened is that the nails began to rust, since the Embassy was right next to the Indian Ocean. Over the course of time the nails completely rusted out, causing a cascade of tiles to come shooting off the roof and crashing down right next to the main entrance of the Chancery. The noise was so load that the President's security detail up the street at her residence thought that our Embassy had been bombed and rushed to provide assistance. What was truly fortunate was that no one was coming or going out of the Chancery at the time as they would have been flattened and killed by the mass of tiles that came down. Almost half the roof surface was gone and when I left Colombo for the second time, Foreign Buildings was still trying to figure out a fix to the roof.

2001: Kigali, Rwanda: Kigali is a small sleepy town whose claim to fame or infamy is the 1994 Rwandan Genocide of between 500,000 to 1,000,000 people when the Tutsi and Hutu people slaughtered each other throughout the country. Almost everyone you talk to at either our Embassy, the hotel, or in town had some family member killed during this fighting. The events were depicted in the movie "Hotel Rwanda" and the main tourists' attractions around Kigali are sights where people had been slaughtered and their bones are now on display. When I was offered tours of these areas I politely declined citing some embassy work that needed my attention. The other big attraction was gorilla watching in the north, however, at the time I was TDY to Kigali, the Ambassador had put the sites off limits due to fighting along the border. The only other thing that sticks in my mind about Kigali was the hotel and restaurant. Think it was an Intercon Hotel and the restaurant was situated outside by the swimming pool. Most meals were decent and I didn't get sick eating there. ALMOST! I was TDY for about 6 weeks and every night I watched people at the hotel eating beautiful looking Chef's Salads and everyone seemed to be enjoying them. Now, I know better than to eat raw vegetables in Africa and I usually stay away from non-cooked items. But I thought, everyone else is eating them, they look so good, surely the hotel takes precautions in preparing vegetables and salads, so why not try one. Bad Move! Don't think I have to describe in vivid detail what happened the next day other than saying I didn't venture too far from the toilet at the Embassy or my hotel.

2002: Cotonou, Benin: If I said that Kigali was a small, sleepy town, I can only say that Benin was an even smaller and sleepier place. The Embassy was situated down a side street and surrounded by a large farmers market. The first day the driver took me to work I thought the guy didn't know where I was headed. No, I'm not going to the market to shop, I'm going to work. Then all of a sudden there was a DS approved vehicle drop bar on the horizon and embassy guards and bingo, our embassy. When I saw this all I could think was, "The terrorists will never find this place, not with the market on almost all four sides." Great security! Benin is a bit of a blur. I remember going one night to dinner at a super nice restaurant located down by the docks. There you are driving through the docks and again wondering if the person you were with knows where the hell he is going. Then presto again, there is a small street section with a beautiful restaurant and a disco next to it, all lit up and spectacular looking. When you see it you think to yourself, "Am I back in Washington, D.C. and going to Georgetown?" Maybe the rents around the docks were cheaper, but definitely a strange location but as the night progressed the crowds convened on the scene and the restaurant and disco soon filled.

The only other thing that sticks in my mind about Cotonou was sitting outside the hotel by the swimming pool at night and having a drink and a cigar. My entertainment for the evening was watching a lone rat doing laps around the swimming pool and later vanishing somewhere, hopefully not back into the hotel itself. Does nightlife get any more exciting than this? I think not.

2002: The World Summit, Johannesburg, South Africa: I was picked to be the main coordinator for DS at The World Summit, which had several thousand attendees, including an American Delegation of close to 1,000. The event was also attended by our Secretary of State and we also had a number of VIPs to provide coverage to. The Summit went off without a hitch, however, the South Africans had their act together as far as security goes. Unmanned drones watched the crowds and avenues where marches were planned and when people did get close to sites where an event was taking place, there were lots of police including mounted police. There is nothing like a police officer on a gigantic horse to get people out of the way. Think the only delegate incident involved some delegates who tried picking up some prostitutes and ended up getting rolled. South Africa is very deceiving to the average visitor. Most of the cities are very modern and remind you of being in Virginia or some place in the U.S. Nice stores and street side cafes. Perfectly safe during the daytime but come back at night and it is completely different story. You have a 50%, or greater, chance of getting robbed or mugged, or both. I tried to explain this to our delegation during an arrival briefing, however, most of them must have thought I was blowing smoke out of my ass. Almost all our homes at the Embassy and our Consulates have armed guards at night because of the high rate of robbery and crime in the country. That's in addition to barred windows, reinforced doors, alarm and panic alarm systems, and safe havens in all our houses.

2003: Sanaa, Yemen: When I arrived at Sanaa all the dependents had been evacuated from the Embassy and there were perhaps 13 State Employees besides numerous Special Ops folks there, all TDY like myself. Almost all the American TDYers were housed at one of the local hotels and the place was like a fortress with a small contingent of local police and military assigned to protect it; complete with 50 cals. mounted on jeeps around the compound. The first morning that I was there I went down to the restaurant for breakfast and was amazed that almost everyone there was wearing a fishing type vest. I sat there looking at these people and wondered to myself why everyone was dressed to go fishing. I thought back to my reading on Yemen before I left for post and didn't remember any of the tourist guides saying there was great trout fishing or really any kind of good fishing in this desert country. After I got checked into the Embassy and was issued a handgun and talked with folks I came to realize that the vests were to cover up your gun and not a fishing accessory like I first had thought. Turns out, if you were in Yemen, you better have a gun with you.

There wasn't a whole lot of after-hours things to do in town mainly because of the tribal and terrorist threat that existed. The Marines at the Embassy had Happy Hours after work 3-4 times a week and most nights someone would come into the Marine House and drop $200-$300 on the bar and announce that the drinks were on the house until the money ran out. Think in the 5-6 weeks I was there I bought maybe 3-4 drinks and the rest was covered by TDYers from one organization or another.

The other entertainment, along with a Chinese and French restaurant at our hotel, was the nightclub on the roof of the hotel. Again, almost all TDY folks with a few local couples popping in now and then. Usually a local couple would come in, the women in a Berka, the Islamic top to bottom covering for women, and upon getting seated the women could discard the Berka and be wearing T-shirts and tight blue jeans. They'd party and drink and then don the Berka when it was time to leave.

Entertainment at the club would vary but mostly consisted of the Russian Belly Dancers, a mother and her two daughters who would put on a nightly show for all the Americans who frequented the club. Also available, cheap drinks and Cuban cigars. One night while watching the dancers I was sitting with some Special Ops guy who commented," Hey, Russian Belly Dancers, good scotch and Cuban cigars, It don't get any better than this. You know, if it wasn't for the fuckin terrorists, this would be a pretty good place to live."

Fortunately my TDY was fairly uneventful except for a prison break that took place in which a number of terrorist suspects managed to escape. There may have also been a demonstration or two against the U.S. but nothing major. A week or two after I got home, however, there was a large demonstration at our Embassy and when the police couldn't control the crowd they decided to crank up the .50 caliber machine on the jeep just outside our entrance gate. The demonstration ended and people dispersed after the police opened fire with the machine gun and killed a number of the demonstrators.

2003: Lome, Togo: Now here's a country that's not on the tourist routes. Another small and fairly quiet African country sandwiched between Benin and Ghana on the Gulf of Guinea. Fishing and a large seaport are two of the major industries there. Fortunately the GSO was an avid golfer and we managed to play at one of the local clubs every weekend and on holidays while I was there. I rented a set of clubs that I think were left there by Sam Snead or some golf legend as they were probably older than me but they played pretty well. We usually played at the Golf Club du Togo that had its own PGA tour pro, who had just become the first person ever from Togo to have qualified and played in the British Open. We played a few rounds with him and even though I thought I could hit a drive fairly far, he would outdrive us by 75-100 yards with little effort. Lots of fun and a very nice guy. We also had young boys who caddied for us and I was amazed that after only one round of golf, this 12 year old kid could correctly pick the club that I would normally use after just seeing me play just once. A few times I questioned his chose and asked him for a different club. He merely rolled his eyes and when my choose turned out to be wrong, gave me the look that said, " You dumb shit, I told you what club to use!" The course was pretty good for Africa and had grass fairways and rolled and oiled sand greens. I had played before on sand greens but never firmly rolled and oiled ones. My caddy eyed my ball and told me how my ball would break on its way to the hole. I thought to myself, sand greens Don't Break! Wrong, sure as could be the ball broke just like my caddy said it would and he eye me for not listening to his advice. I soon began to listen faithfully to the caddy and accepted whatever club he offered and putted just like he told me. The end result, a better game and lower score.

It's funny because I've golfed in several other African countries and the level of the courses can vary like night and day. Some fairways are sand and weeds and if you hit your drive within boundaries you can tee up your ball for the second shot. Most had sand greens although a few had some sort of grass. The thing is that no matter how bad a golf course was in some country there are always people who played on it. Beggars can't be choosers. Caddies also vary from country to country. My caddy in Togo was great and I would love to have him here in the U.S. carrying my bag. Other caddies will constantly say,

"Good shot, good shot!" That's even it you hit the ball out of bounds or into the lake. It's still a good shot. They also always have extra balls on them that they will gladly sell you should you lose your ball. I even had caddy take off his shoes and climb a palm tree to retrieve my golf ball from the top of it. They clean your clubs and shoes when you're done and will have a coke with you after 18 holes. I still remember the caddies in Beijing, China. They were young girls in bib-overalls with sunbonnets and white gloves and they carried your bag, said good shot, good shot, but only when it was a good shot but didn't choose your clubs for you. When they finished caddying for the day and the guys were having a beer at the clubhouse you would see them on the driving range with little baskets, all in a line, collecting the balls that had been hit during the day. No machines there to pick up the golf balls.

There weren't many good restaurants by the house I was staying in but there was a decent Chinese Restaurant just around the corner which I frequented so much that the owner told me that I, and my friends, got a 20% discount whenever we ate there because I was such a good customer. Two things I've learned about eating overseas after visiting so many countries. The First, leave a good and big tip for the country you're in and whenever you go back to that restaurant you'll be treated like a king. It never fails, especially in the poorer countries where tipping is often not done. The Second thing I've learned is that no matter where you travel: Europe, Asia, Middle East, South America, Africa, etc, there will ALWAYS be a Chinese and an Italian Restaurant somewhere in the town you are in. And they're usually pretty good. I remember my TDY to Zambia that I mentioned. The waitress continually told me to go to the Italian buffet on Wednesday night for the entire time I was there. I thought to myself, how good can Italian be in Zambia? The last week I was in Zambia, the witness told me she wasn't going to serve me and that I HAD TO eat upstairs or not eat. So off to the Italian buffet. It was out of sight! All kinds of Italian cold cuts and cheeses, homemade desserts, pasta sauces made to order on the spot by the chefs and homemade pasta. Turns out both chefs had trained for a year in Italy on how to cook Italian food and did a splendid job doing it. The only bad thing about this was the fact that it was my last week in Zambia and I wouldn't get another chance to eat there. On another night my waitress at this same hotel insisted that I try crocodile as it was delicious. PASS! Again she told me, either try it or you won't eat here tonight. Turned out it was delicious grilled. People always laugh when they ask you what it tasted like. You know the answer already. CHICKEN!

2004: Vientiane, Laos: Laos is perhaps one of the few countries that your average tourist has never heard of or had no desire to visit. It is, however, a great place to visit and when I was there it was one of the safer cities in the area. The government was Communist and street and general crime were very low because of the government's tight grip on society. What amazed me too were the large number of young women backpacking through the country, both by themselves or in groups of two or three, and staying at local hostels without any fear of being accosted. Everywhere you looked they were hiking around and I thought to myself that you would never see this back in the United States because single women wouldn't feel this safe traveling on their own like this.

Vientiane is located a very short distance from the Peace Bridge which separates Laos and Thailand. During the Viet Nam War our Embassy became a hub of activity as many of the government organizations that couldn't operate elsewhere, chose Laos as their base of operations. The Embassy staff swelled to several hundred. The Embassy staff had since shrunk down to almost nothing although DEA still had a strong presence there. Many of Thai people travel to Laos to visit Luang Prabang that many say is how Thailand used to be way back when. The Mekong River runs through Vientiane and there are an abundance of Buddhist Temples and Shrines located throughout the area. There are also several market areas where you can buy just about anything, including some great knock off watches for a fraction of the price as the same watch costs in China. I picked up a few of these gems when I was there and when I take them to the jeweler for a battery change, even they don't realize they are knock offs.

I was worried when I arrived there when I found out that the daily per diem, M&IE, for Vientiane was a mere $34 a day. I was used to getting $100 or more a day for meals and incidentals and wondered how I could possibly eat and drink for just $34 a day. Well, let me tell you, it was dirt cheap eating there. I found a Great Italian Restaurant and the tab for an appetizer, main course, some vino and perhaps a dessert if I was very hungry, was about $14, which included the tip. There was also a very good German restaurant close by as well as a Danish bakery that was out of sight. One restaurant caught my eye, Snow White and One Dwarf, however, I'm not sure why I never tried it to see just what they were serving.

The Embassy itself was an old, quiet place, a remnant
of the Viet Nam War and as I mentioned the staff levels
had dwindled to just your key section people. Not a lot
happened during my TDY although one day we did have
an interesting incident. I had just finished breakfast and
was walking to the Embassy when my cell phone went off
and upon answering it I was informed that there was a
large fire in progress at the Embassy and that I better haul
ass and get there. Off I ran and fortunately was almost
there already. When I arrived I saw a number of fire
trucks and some of the Marines at one of the annex
buildings, which was on an adjoining compound behind
the Embassy Chancery. I came to learn that a fire had
broken out in the building and that the smoke and flames
were not visible to the guards at the main gate to the
compound. Fortunately there was an apartment building
across the street from the annex and a concerned person
called the front gate guards to ask them if they were aware
that one of our buildings was burning down. This caught
the guards by surprise since they had no idea what was
happening and finally the fire department was summoned
and they quickly extinguished the flames but not before
several rooms were burnt out and there was a lot of smoke
and water damage. Can't remember what the cause was
but seem to remember that bad wiring was probably the
culprit. So that was the major incident during this TDY.
Seems like building fires are quite common in the Foreign
Service. Can't remember if I mentioned it but we also
had a small fire at the Main Building of the State
Department when I headed the Domestic Operations
Division and I did mention the fire at the Annex Building
in New Delhi. There was also a famous fire in Paris in

which one unfortunate Marine Guard fell to his death while trying to fight the fire at the Embassy. After that incident Marines were prohibited from trying to contain fires at Embassies unless there was the possibility of the loss of lives.

2007: Monrovia, Liberia: This was an entirely new type of assignment for both DS and me. I was not being assigned as a TDY RSO to the Embassy but rather would be a Special Advisor to the President of Liberia. Charles Taylor ruled Liberia from 1997 until 2003 when he was brought up on charges of War Crimes and Crimes Against Humanity by a Special Court in Sierra Leone. He was involved in the Civil War in Sierra Leone from 1991 until 2002 and before that was a guerrilla leader in Liberia's first Civil War that lasted through the 1990s. A second civil war would take place from 1999 to 2003 when people rebelled against Taylor and his government. Part of this war was depicted in the Hollywood movie, "Lord of War" and while I was in Liberia I was given a DVD done by a British news reporter, who chronicled Taylor and his "Children Soldiers" and some of the crimes they committed during this period. Children aged 12 yrs. and older could be seen with AK-47s shooting innocent civilians and chopping off men's arms at either the shoulder or elbow. They would ask the captured person if he wanted a long sleeve(arm chopped off at the shoulder) or a short sleeve (arm chopped off at the elbow). All the while the youths cheered and laughed while they carried out these atrocities. Taylor and some members of his crew would eventually be arrested in 2006 while in Nigeria and later stand trail and be convicted by a Special Court in Sierra Leone. When I was doing my TDY in

Liberia both Taylor's wife and a good number of his former soldiers still lived in Monrovia not far from the Liberian government buildings. His nephew was also very active in the Liberian Government and was a continual opponent of the current President on many issues she tried to push forward. The United Nations eventually sent a large military contingent to Liberia to help maintain peace and stability. They were there in 2007, however, a move was under way for their eventual withdrawal.

In 2005 Ellen Johnson Sirleaf would be elected the First Female Head of State in Africa and assume the role of President of Liberia. She would later be reelected President in 2011 and in that same year received the Nobel Peace Prize. So it was in 2007 that I first met this exceptional woman and would become an advisor to her on security matters and ensuring that her security detail was adequately trained to protect this high profile figure. After she was first elected President, Diplomatic Security sent a full protective detail and equipment to Liberia to protect her and began to train her prospective security detail. If I remember correctly they would remain in country for close to a year before handing over the reins to her local detail. When I arrived in Liberia she was being protected by the Nigerian Secret Service, which truly surprised me since I just assumed she would have a Liberian Security Detail. When I discussed the situation with a number of people I would learn that the President had fears that some of Taylor's sympathizers would get on her detail and try to assassinate her. It was decided to use the Nigerians for a time to do all the close-in protection on her. Liberians would only be on the outer security circle and some would carry only unloaded weapons for fear that they might be turned on her. After I got the full story I saw that I had an extremely hard job ahead of me in both convincing the President that eventually she had to rely on her own people and ensuring that everyone could be trusted. The United Nations also provided security coverage for all the President's moves and I explained to her that the UN wouldn't be there forever and that it was time to become self sufficient. I decided that I needed to accompany her daily on all her moves and see how her detail performed and where I could improve on things. First thing was to get them some better equipment from our folks and then train the detail in its use. The Assistant RSO and I then spent many a day at the range showing everyone how to shoot correctly and how to do protective moves with a VIP.

Some of her people were very good as they had previously been trained by DS, however, there were others you did not want to be close to if the shit hit the fan, as you would possibly get shot by them instead of the bad guys. One person shot the ground out about 6' ahead of her and another held the handgun like a rapper in an American movie. When I asked what the hell he was doing he said that was how all the folks in the movies did it.

Finally after several weeks of training, yelling and one on one with everyone, I was a bit happier that these guys would do what they were trained to do. One thing I was particularly sure of was the fact that most of them would gladly lay down their lives to save their President. Most of the agents were not very old and many had only a high school education, if that, but they were dedicated. The Director of the Security Service was born in Liberia, educated in the United States and lived there, until he decided that he had to come back to Liberia and do something for his country. This would be true of a large number of people in government and industry there. Liberia and the United States had close ties going all the way back to the days of slaves in the U.S. Our government would provide major support for this country. We even printed their currency in the U.S. for them.

A few years before my arrival the President's residence was housed in the Ministry Building and mysteriously caught fire while the President was hosting a reception there. Fortunately everyone was evacuated and no one was killed or injured. The President and all her staff were convinced that Taylor sympathizers were responsible although nothing was every developed to prove this. The Chinese came forward and offered to rebuild not only the Ministry Building but to build a new Olympic style stadium in town. I should add that many of the downtown areas and bridges in Monrovia were still in ruins from previous civil wars and that it was odd to see a new and modern stadium sitting in the middle of an otherwise war torn downtown area. It's funny because the Chinese have been on a campaign of sorts in building stadiums throughout Africa. I can think of close to a dozen cities I have visited who have had stadiums erected by the Chinese. The Chinese were also very active in offering the President's Office equipment and training for her protective detail. I was once approached by our Ambassador who voiced his displeasure about this and my response was, "If you don't want the Chinese to give them equipment and guns you better get with Washington and have them give you equipment for everyone." No response by him on that one. The other thing that I found a bit strange, or maybe even humorous, was the fact that after the Ministry Building was completed a small building was erected just behind it and two Chinese looking gentlemen sat there daily, doing what I don't know, but I had a few suspicions.

The TDY in Liberia lasted about 8 weeks and I think there was a marked improvement in the security detail's overall performance, however, there were a few interesting and perhaps funny incidents during this period. The President was driven around town in a newish Mercedes sedan or SUV while the security detail followed in some old and high mileage vehicles that sometimes made the journey and sometimes broke down along the way. One day we were en route somewhere when the follow car stopped running. I was in the first follow car with the Director and three other agents. The Director tells the other 6 agents to pile into our car as he wants everyone at the event site. That puts about 12 people into a vehicle designed for 5-6 maximum. I have two agents sitting on top of me while the others are jammed into every corner of the vehicle. So there I sit thinking to myself, "What if we get attacked right now, I can't even get to my gun!" We get to the site without incident and I later ream out the Director for piling everyone into the car and making us completely ineffective if something would have happened. This however goes on deaf ears and he feels that having everyone in the car was the better move and Oh Yes, since he was siting in the front seat without anyone on his lap he could have repelled an attack. OK! I later send an e-mail back to Headquarters asking people "How many people can you pile into a Toyota SUV?" Answer: 12!

The UN Peacekeepers provided the motorcade and site security for all the President's moves. Anywhere between 30 to 60 soldiers, from a variety of different countries, were stationed at the sites we went to and this at least gave the appearance of a security presence. The main problem with using UN personnel was that you might have 5 guys from Pakistan, 6 from India, 2 from Europe somewhere, 10 from different countries in Africa and no one could talk to each other because most Did Not speak any English. Added to this was the fact that the UN normally didn't assign an NCO or Officer-in- Charge for these groups. Groups were briefed separately before heading to their destination and they showed up at the site at the designated time, did their duty at the site and left at a predetermined time. This would have been fine if the President was always punctual and on time everywhere. Unfortunately, this was not the case with Mrs. President and she constantly ran anywhere from 30 minutes to an hour behind schedule for almost every move she made. The result was thus. The UN folks would show up at say 1:00 pm and had been told to stay on site until 3:00 p.m., when they were instructed to leave. The President would show up at say 2:00 to 2:30 p.m. and at 3:00 p.m. the soldiers would all begin to leave even though she was still in the midst of her speech. When I see what was happening I told one of my guys to get down there and get with their commander and tell them that they can't leave yet. He went to address the problem and came back only to tell me that they had no one commanding the troops and that they were told to leave at 3:00 p.m. and

219

by god that was what they were doing, no matter what we told them. So we suddenly we went from about 50 guys protecting the President to just 10 of my guys, as the UN troops march in an orderly or disorderly manner back to their base. You've got to love doing security in some of these countries.

The other thing the detail did, regardless of how many times I yelled at them for it, was to send out the Lead vehicle that was equipped with a PA system, and then one of the persons in the car would yell to the slow traffic that the President was coming and that they should, and I quote, " Get out of the way, Get the Fuck out of the Way!" The first time this happened I thought I was hearing things until the lead car made the announcement again. I did speak to the detail and the regular traffic cops and tried to explain to them that it wasn't very cool to be yelling, "Get the FUCK out of the way", especially when it was the President and her motorcade. I wish I could say that this problem got fixed but it continued to pop up now and then when traffic got congested and the lead car had to move folks out of our way. Imagine if you were running a detail in the U.S. and our Lead started making that announcement whenever traffic got heavy, especially if it was the President's motorcade.

The last thing that happened during my TDY was that the President of China came to Liberia for the first time in history and we hosted a very large outdoor dinner for him and his staff. Also in attendance was Queen Noor of Jordan along with her traveling companion. This was interesting for me as Queen Noor was the first VIP I had even protected when she visited Washington, D.C., way back when. I was going to go over and tell her this but then thought I would be dating both her and I and I wasn't sure she wanted to be reminded about how many years ago this really was.

So after about 8 weeks I left Liberia and headed home while the Liberian President headed to Washington, D.C. to address Congress and see her close friend, Secretary Rice.

2005: Busan, Korea-APEC 2005 KOREA: For a time I was fortunate enough to be chosen by the Department to be the lead coordinator for a number of high level conferences that took place throughout the world. In 2005 I first traveled to Seoul, Korea and then took their bullet train down to Busan, which lies to the South and on the ocean. APEC 2005 was a meeting of all the world leaders and my job was to coordinate things between visiting U.S. dignitaries and our Embassy and the Koreans. The event went off without fanfare and there were only some minor problems. The Koreans had brought in large numbers of police and military to provide security and fortunately there was only one roadway leading into the peninsula where the Summit was held. Once the Summit got underway the police erected a large wall of conex containers across the roadway to prevent any demonstrations from getting close to the venue. Just to be safe they also installed water canons on the top of the wall that they eventually did get to use while repelling a crowd of demonstrators after the Summit got underway. The only other incident I became involved in with concerned a person from an outside agency who decided one evening to test the security at one of the hotels that several VIPs were staying at. He was convinced that the police weren't checking the photos on the IDs and so he borrowed a friend's badge and tried to enter the hotel where several Heads of State were staying. Low and behold, he was amazed when the police immediately spotted the illegal ID and he got himself arrested despite trying to talk his way out of the situation. I received a late night telephone call and headed to town to try to resolve the situation and get the guy released. Fortunately I was successful but did make of point of chewing out both the arrested individual and his boss who had dreamed up this silly stunt. The cops may have looked like they were slacking off but they weren't as he found out.

2008: The Green Zone, Baghdad, Iraq: After the Iraqi War got rolling I was always curious how it was over there and in 2008 I got to go there to help our security office with some projects. After flying for hours to Kuwait and then finally getting into Baghdad by military air we landed at Zero Dark Thirty and then had to wait several hours to get to the Embassy after we found out that the helicopters that were to get us into town were grounded because of a sand storm. At some ungodly hour we boarded a Rhino, which was specially armored bus and traveled the ten miles or so under heavy guard, finally arriving in the Green Zone and one of Saddam Hussein's many palaces, which is where I set up office with the rest of the DS Agents. The Palace and the Green Zone were occupied at that time by the State Department contingent and hundreds of military personnel, mostly over the rank of Captain and had more full bird Colonels than I knew the military ever had. I worked in the Palace itself and slept in one of the many grand living quarters that consisted of a small trailer, divided into two bedrooms, with a bath in the middle. Each unit had a bed that had seen it's better days and looked like an elephant had slept in it as the mattress was now about a half inch thick, a dresser, wardrobe and a small TV which did get some good American shows. The trailers were surrounded by about 3'-4' of sandbags in an attempt to protect them from the frequent rocket attacks that made it into the Green Zone daily. About 2 weeks before I arrived two guys had been killed when the rockets hit outside their trailers and despite having the air raid siren sounding an attack, both gentlemen decided to just lay in bed and were hit by flying projectiles from the rockets. We had a rocket launch detection system in place at our Command Center that could see rockets entering the Green Zone and then the "Big Voice" would start sounding throughout the compounds and say, "Incoming, Incoming, Duck and Cover." When you heard this announcement you had about thirty-seconds to get to cover if you were outside or to roll out of your bed, throw on body armor or at least get it over part of you, and then lay there and count to thirty. If, at the end of your thirty count you were still there and in one piece, you could get up and resume what you were doing. The first 2-3 weeks there it seemed like every night, when you were really sleeping well, the Big Voice would start sounding and you would wake up and after you realized where the fuck you were and what was happening, you'd roll and pray, since you had already expended 15-20 seconds of your 30 second time limit before the rockets hit. Many of the folks who had been there for a while just ignored the Big Voice and kept doing what they were doing although like I just mentioned, occasionally someone did get killed. I remember one day at the gym the Big Voice came on and the guy on the treadmill to my right leaped off and hit the ground, while the guy on my left continued his running and just watched the other people hitting the ground. I think I just kept going as it just looked too goofy to leap off the treadmill and try to hide under it. I thought better safe than sorry most times but sometimes figured a rocket hitting where I was would destroy the whole building so I might as well just go with the flow.

Saddam's Palace was a large, ornate building complete with surrounding gardens and a large swimming pool in the back. Inside, the walls and ceilings had paintings of various subjects. Two pictures in particular stick in my mind. One painting on the ceiling was a huge Stallion rearing up on his hindquarters with clouds surrounding him. The second was on a wall and pictured a series of scud missiles firing out over the city. A stark contrast from the first picture. I remember entering one of the bathrooms when I first arrived and seeing about 25-30 individual toilet stalls along one wall plus about two dozen sinks to the rear. As I mentioned, most of the U.S. staff and military worked at this Palace in the Green Zone although the new Embassy compound was nearing completion.

The new Embassy compound was over 100 acres in size and had numerous buildings. There was the Chancery and Annex Buildings where the majority of the offices were, in addition to several staff apartment buildings, an indoor swimming pool and gym, cafeteria and even a school. I thought the school was kind of strange as it appears that someone thought the conflict in Iraq would be long over by the time the Embassy opened and that dependents and children would be coming back to Iraq with the State Department staff. Eventually the school was converted into more offices as I guess everyone finally realized that it would be a long, long time before children would ever return to Baghdad. They were also planning to add another 20 acres to the existing compound and expectations then were that there would be several thousand employees, making it one of the largest U.S. Embassies in the world. Initially hundreds of State Department employees volunteered for positions there as you were paid your regular salary plus 40% Danger Pay and since there wasn't much to spend money on you saved LOTS of money. This would later change and eventually the State Department had to draft people, many times against their will, to be assigned there. The glamour had worn off by then for most people. You also received your meals, housing and laundry as part of the deal. A year of assignment in Iraq was like spending two years or more somewhere else without danger pay.

Speaking of meals. You ate very well in Baghdad during your stay, to say the least. One night was steak night-made to order, another lobster night-all you could eat, turkey, meats, Spanish meals, you name it, they had it. There was a cake and pie station with dozens of baked goodies. There was even a Haagen Daaz ice cream station with every flavor and topping you could imagine. Meals consisted of breakfast, lunch, dinner and a midnight snack if you still had room in your stomach. Most people permanently assigned there for a year put on a few pounds, if not many pounds during their stay. Two day laundry and dry cleaning service was also available for free and most people received a cell phone when they arrived that could used to call home, at no charge, whoever you wanted to talk: loved ones or just shoot the shit with a friend or girl friend. It Was Not bad duty there although you still could get killed or messed up if you weren't careful. Initially most people figured it was worth the risk as the assignments were only one year or less.

The time finally came when State Department wanted to transition from the Palace to the new compound. The only problem was that no one wanted to move from the Palace as the new compound didn't have all the meal and laundry facilities that people had become accustomed to. Meals were a little less elaborate there and the number of people residing to move into the new staff apartments was minimal. Eventually the Ambassador decreed that everyone would move and immediately! One thing that didn't initially get done when the compound was being finished up was landscaping. It seems that the money had begun to dry up for this project and so instead of a nicely treed and flowered compound, there was only sand, sand and more sand everything. When the winds blew you couldn't see two feet in front of you because of the flying sand. Entrances to the buildings had mounds of sand against them and had to be constantly swept out.

The lack of movement to the new compound also included most of my DS comrades and so I would eventually move over to the new compound and become the senior security officer there as everyone else wanted to remain at the Palace. I did volunteer one junior Agent to come with me and we assumed security control at the new facilities. I must say I wasn't too impressed by the workmanship at the compound as some of the buildings were already beginning to fall apart before anyone had moved in. Part of the facade of the Annex Building even fell off a week before the Ambassador was to dedicate the compound. Some of the security equipment was not what I would have picked for this facility either. Everyone thought the war and fighting would be long over when we finally moved in.

The President just recently had to station several hundred Marines at the Embassy to provide protection to its limited staff as the war continues to ravage Baghdad. Many of the staff have been ordered to depart the Embassy as it has become too dangerous for people to be there. Even though I know how much the final tab was for this Embassy, I will not put that down in writing as I'm afraid it would blow your mind and have many people writing their Representatives to complain about how our government is spending their money.

There were only 2-3 rocket attacks while I was working at the new compound as one of the clerics in Baghdad had declared a cease-fire and all of a sudden there were no rocket attacks for the rest of my stay there. That was even scarier than when there were daily attacks as you got this idea in the back of your head that the bad guys were sitting somewhere and dreaming up bad shit to do to us. We also had a project of putting huge concrete barriers all around the buildings at the compound as we came to realize that our buildings weren't built to withstand the riggers of war and that military rockets could cause severe damage to even hardened buildings. The Texas Barriers, as they were called, were built locally and we ordered 100s and 100s of them to surround all the buildings in the compound and to line some streets that were frequently traveled by us. The company making and selling them must have made a fortune since I think one barrier cost over $500 and we used thousands of them all over the city.

My stay in Baghdad went by quickly as we usually worked over ten hours a day since there was very little entertainment there besides eating, going to the gym or swimming pool or reading. If there was any partying going on I wasn't aware of it or invited.

So after two months in sandy Baghdad I was back on a C-130 military aircraft, which incidentally came from South Carolina (where I now lived) to fly us part of the way home. Mission accomplished and I was one of the few people, besides our military, who got to see Iraq first hand while the war was supposedly winding down.

2009: COP 15 World Leaders Meeting, Copenhagen, Denmark: In 2009 the UN hosted a World Leaders meeting in Copenhagen, which focused on the environment and global warming. Over 130 World Leaders attended the main meeting along with numerous delegations from around the world. The U.S. Delegation consisted of members of Congress and the Senate and included Senator Kerry, Nancy Pelosi, New York Mayor Bloomberg, Governor Schwarzenegger, Secretary of State Clinton and numerous other VIPs. My role was to coordinate things for all the arriving delegations, get people IDs and gun permits from the UN Security Staff and just be there to do whatever someone asked me to do. I frequently got these types of assignments and figured there would be several people from the Embassy to assist me, only to find out that I was The Man and everything seemed to end up with me. It was fun though as I got to escort many of the VIPs and coordinate their activities at the conference site where the meetings were held. The anarchists had gone public and said that they would march on the site when all the World Leaders had assembled and "Burn the Place Down!" That got everyone's attention and there was a huge security presence at the conference site. I can't think of many meetings, other than the United Nations, where that many Heads of State were present at one time and at the same location. The police had drones flying around to monitor activities and the Danish had just passed some creative legislation before the conference that caught everyone's eye. The new laws allowed police officers to detain or arrest anyone who remotely looked like a troublemaker even if he wasn't doing anything illegal. So if I was walking down the street and a police officer looked at me and thought to himself, "He looks like an Troublemaker", he could detain me for 24 hours, no questions asked. As the conference progressed, that is exactly what they began to do. One night while a demonstration was underway in the downtown shopping area, numerous people were detained, flex cuffed and made to sit on the freezing ground to wait for buses that would haul them off to a detention area. Unfortunately the buses took a very long time to get there and several people got very cold asses and some even pissed themselves when they couldn't hold it any longer. The next day the press had a field day with both the incident and the new laws that were in place.

Although the anarchists continually threatened to invade the conference they never managed to do so. The fact that the site was several miles from downtown and required either auto and metro transportation to get there made it easy for the police to monitor people coming and going. A few demonstrations did take place downtown but with the newly passed legislation the police were quick to round up troublemakers as the new law gave them increased powers that most police departments usually don't have.

I was able to get Governor Schwarzenegger to do a photo op with both the Embassy Marines and the UN Security Staff and so I was golden whenever I had a favor to get from either. It was interesting that the UN Security Office had determined that Governor Schwarzenegger had a higher profile than many World Leaders and so the security afforded him by the UN Security Staff was larger than some World Leaders from smaller countries and they gave him the same amount of UN Coverage at the conference site as they gave our President. I was with him as he did a few TV interviews and I must say that he was better versed than many World Leaders when it came to the environment and global warming.

The meeting went by without any major incidents although several people did get arrested or detained the week the event took place. What also cut down on the numbers at the demonstrations was the fact that it was colder than hell in Copenhagen at the time and even managed to snow a few days. Only the hearty anarchists came out while the average person decided to go someplace a little warmer.

2010: Toronto, Canada, G20 Summit Meeting: The G20 was a meeting of world leaders in Toronto to discuss the world economy. Several Heads of State attended and I was again selected to liaison between the Canadians and the U.S. delegation who attended the Summit. Numerous demonstrations were planned and law enforcement was on the alert for anarchists who might be traveling from the United States as one of the last G20 Summits in Seattle, Washington, had numerous demonstrations resulting in major property damage throughout that city. The Toronto Police had set up a temporary detention center at former movie studio lot to house anyone who got arrested during the Summit. Police and military were stationed at strategic locations throughout the city.

On the opening days of the Summit and before many of the Heads of State had arrived in Toronto, a large demonstration took place and winded through the downtown area. Police were on high alert for trouble and anarchists had managed to infiltrate the crowd and as the crowd approached the downtown shopping area the anarchists took off their jackets and shirts revealing their traditional black outfits while donning various items to cover the faces and identities. The anarchists then smashed store and business windows although several businesses had taken precautions and boarded up their windows before hand. They also set a number of police vehicles on fire and when I finally got back to my hotel that night a burnt out police car was about 40' from the entrance of my hotel. In all over a million dollars in damages were reported that day. Surprisingly the police were slow to respond to the situation and only a hand full of persons were arrested that day. It seems that the anarchists later donned new clothes after their rampage ended and then mingled with the more peaceful demonstrations, thus avoiding detection and arrest.

On the days that followed however, the police began a major campaign of arresting both disorderly and many times peaceful demonstrators. On a number of occasions the police instructed demonstrators to disperse and many did, only to be arrested almost immediately. As I and the security people at the Embassy watched the happenings on television we couldn't understand or believe some of the people the police were arresting as they didn't appear to have broken any laws. In all over 1500 persons were arrested and detained in the city's makeshift jail on the outskirts of town. The press had a field day with the arrests since as I mentioned some of them did not make any sense. It was also reported that the conditions at the detention center were terrible and people didn't have immediate access to many things. Citizens were outraged by the damage the town sustained and the overall cost of the G20 and the G8 Summit, which had been held a week before, which was said to have run almost $1 Billion Dollars. They also were appalled by the response of the police in being slow to arrest people initially and then arresting anyone who looked like they might cause trouble. Several parts of the town were closed to the public and a number of major sporting events had to be either cancelled or relocated, adding to the frustration that the people already had.

Demonstrations and minor incidents took place throughout the span of the Summit and after people started to depart the city, parts of Toronto looked like a war zone. Several lawsuits were also in the works as I prepared to head home. The Toronto Police were criticized for their actions and their Police Chief was being asked to resign by the citizens of the city.

That about sums up some of my more interesting TDYs I had as a WAE. I've done a few more assignments but nothing really interesting or exciting took place during those trips. I continue to be on the WAE roles and to go out ion assignments whenever the Department has a need for me.

EPILOGUE

I guess that sums up what I've been up to for the past 40 or more years and what I've been doing for the Government. I know many people still don't believe me when I tell them I worked and still work for the U.S.Department of State. They're still convinced that I work for the CIA or some black ops type organization. I plan to continue working for the Government for as long as I am in good health and have that desire to see new places and things. I've also started to do contract work for the State Department's Antiterrorism Assistance Program (ATA). I hope that you've enjoyed my book and again I would remind you that this was the Government 30-40 years ago. Today our Agents are more disciplined and don't do the stupid things we did back in the 1970's. DS is one of the best, if not the best, law enforcement agency in the world today and our Special Agents are on the front lines fighting terrorism both domestically and overseas. They are the Best of the Best and I am Proud to have been a part of this great organization.

Made in the USA
Middletown, DE
29 March 2016